Reframing Hope

OUR JOURNEY THROUGH CANCER, ADOPTION, AND LOVE

TRAVIS CREASY

WHITNEY CREASY

Romans 8:1

Whitney Creasy
2 Thess. 3:5

CREASY MEDIA
www.travisandwhitney.com

Typesetting and book design by Blackberry Books, Florence, Alabama.

*To my mother, Doris Creasy, affectionately known as "Daw."
You have been a constant source of encouragement and a
loving presence in my life and the lives of my little family.*

*To my babies, Hailee and Daniel. You are a good and perfect
gift to us, and we are blessed to be called your parents. The
resiliency and love for others that I have watched you display
has taught me more than I could ever teach you. Always
remember the promises I have circled for you. Hailee, you are
"a glorious crown, a royal diadem in God's hand, and God's
delight." Daniel, you are "a weapon of righteousness" in the
Kingdom of God.*

Contents

Foreword

ALAN S. BAGGETT, MD

To you, the reader of this book, thank you for engaging and following along with Travis and Whitney on this challenging and perilous expedition.

The reason you have arrived here and are holding this text is almost certainly unique to you, and you alone. No one could have predicted that, here and now, you would be holding these pages and starting on this journey, but God knew. Like all things, God has a continuous and perfect plan in place for you. In moments of crisis or joy, God is there, and He has placed you here for some reason. The challenge is always, to figure out that reason. I imagine that some readers of this book are actively experiencing pain or heartache and are searching for answers and direction. The title *Reframing Hope,* may have resonated strongly with you because your world has recently been jostled and the hope and joy it once held, have disappeared. Perhaps you have been recently diagnosed with cancer or another severe illness, and your life has gone from peaceful and serene to frayed and frazzled. You could be working through the trials and tribulations of fostering or adoption and are in need of guidance and support. Whatever the reason, I firmly believe that this story was intended for you. Hope can be a fickle thing. When unexpected trials present in full force, hope can quickly be dashed and misdirected. It's these trials however that become the nidus for growth, especially the persistence of a bold faith. The first chapter of the New Testament book of James tells us plainly that we should "count it all joy... when you meet trials of various kinds, for you know that the testing of your faith produces steadfastness. And let steadfastness have its full effect, that you may be perfect and complete, lacking in nothing."

Travis and Whitney's path has certainly come with unexpected twists and turns. Their journey has been burdened with fear, heartbreak, and sadness, but their resolve and steadfastness in the faith has only flourished through these trials. I first met Travis and Whitney in October of 2018, just a few days after the word leukemia first entered their personal lexicons. In retrospect, it's a bit odd that Travis and I had never crossed paths prior to that moment. I was raised in a home in the Jacksonburg community in rural north Alabama, less than a half mile from the church Travis and his family attended during his middle school and high school years. We have dozens of mutual friends and back then, ran in similar circles, but our paths never crossed until our overlapping social media networks revealed his illness and admission to the hospital where I work as an internal medicine physician. Given so many mutual ties, I felt compelled to reach out and offer a bedside prayer and provide support if I could. I'll admit that I was a bit worried about what I might be walking into. At this point, I didn't know Travis. I didn't know his precise cancer diagnosis or staging. I didn't know which cancer regimen was going to be initiated or the prognosis of his disease. All I knew before our first meeting was that he was a Christian brother, and this imminent experience was going to be a challenge. Over the next 30 days of hospitalization, Travis and I had the chance to become close friends. We shared books, puzzles and even built a DIY, tabletop catapult to help the time pass. I watched Whitney blossom into the supermom of supermoms, managing the kids at home and supporting her husband at the bedside with humor and love. The real novelty of my experience in all of this was being able to see Travis's faith in action. As the arsenic-based chemotherapy literally poisoned Travis's leukemia cells, I witnessed a persistent joy that could neither be broken nor erased. It's a joy that not all hospitalized patients share. It's a true joy that is rarely expressed in a crisis. When it is present, the care team and hospital staff consistently take notice. Travis's hospital room was adorned with posters and banners from his students. Copied scripture and written prayers were plastered everywhere. It was literally impossible to enter the room without the immediate realization that God was the driver in this place, not the malignancy.

Travis's cancer journey has gone exceedingly well. But one must wonder, what was God's reason for Travis and Whitney's path to dramatically go off on an unexpected and unpredictable tangent? Why did the word cancer have to be thrown into the mix? What was God's plan in all of this?

These questions (or similar inquiries that you are experiencing) may never be completely answered but perhaps, reframing the perspective or our concept of hope can help shed a bit of light on what may feel like a very dark moment in our life.

Was there a nurse who needed to see the joy of the Lord from a family who should otherwise be in turmoil? Was there a Christian physician, who needed to be reminded of who is really in control and see a major trial of faith play out for God's glory? Is there a reader of this book who needs to hear Travis and Whitney's words to help guide them through a chaotic time or prepare them for a future crisis? It is tough to know completely, but I firmly believe that God had and continues to have a plan for the Creasy family, just as He does for you and me. Though the humanly outcome may not always be our personal desire, with the right perspective we can better understand how "in all things God works for the good of those who love him, who have been called according to his purpose" Romans 8:28.

I hope and pray that you find whatever God has in store for you in this book and in each moment of life that lies ahead.

Introduction

This is a book about many things. It's a book about our family, a season of suffering, a season of uncertainty; it's a book about cancer. It's a book about fostering and adoption, and the good and perfect gift of the local church. Most importantly, this is a book about God. This is our story of walking with the Lord through the most challenging season of our life and how we found Him faithful.

We want to let you in on some things we know now that we didn't know before. We learned the local church, the body of Christ, the family of God is important, not just in theory, but in *practicality*. We understand our obedience to God doesn't guarantee an easy or painless life. We are more aware that things are not what they seem, and God is always working behind the scenes for the good of those who love him.

The things we have learned through these experiences have molded and shaped our relationship with God; our relationship with him is different because of our journey. For example, it is easier for us to see suffering as an opportunity for God to make his presence known and for us to grow in faith and endurance. We seek faith in God's goodness and his promises over fear and control. And most importantly, we believe God's nature is compassionate, merciful, slow to anger, abounding in love, forgiving, and just; we filter everything through that lens.

We hope you will feel comfortable joining us on this journey. Our hope in sharing this story is that you will not only learn from our mistakes, but also find peace for the times you feel like your world is spinning out of control. We pray that you find hope in the assurance that God has not forgotten you. We want you to know that it is okay, and even Biblical to mourn and dance at the same time. We anticipate that you will feel a renewed love for and dependence on the Lord's Church as his hands and feet on Earth. Oh, and hopefully you'll get a few laughs too.

CHAPTER 1

Our Story

I guess it's time for an introduction. So here goes.... Hi! I'm Whitney Creasy, and my handsome hubby is Travis. Each day of life with him is an adventure to say the least. He is everything I am not...especially spontaneous and energetic. He is always down for a party, no matter what "important thing" is going on. I'm always going to be the one who feels like we need to stay home and be responsible adults who get the leaves raked up out of the yard, while Travis will never turn down a last-minute trip to Tuscaloosa for a football game in the fall. I believe he makes sure I don't take myself or life too seriously and keeps me young. I would definitely have a lot less fun without him. He teaches me how to celebrate, to cut loose, and to not sweat the small stuff so much.

Travis and I are both total Bible nerds. We can get lost in an N.T. Wright podcast on a road trip really quickly, and we can spend hours in theological discussion over the most peculiar things in scripture. We both teach Bible at Riverside Christian Academy, and Travis preaches at our church on

Sundays, so we spend a good bit of time reading the Bible, and talking about it is one of our favorite pastimes.

***

I'm Travis, Whitney's other half and dad to Hailee and Daniel. Hailee and I are best described by the enneagram personality assessment as "sevens" or as I refer to us "Tiggers." My son is a little less so but still loves to have a good time. We would not get anywhere on time or with the right materials without "My Whitney." She is the woman you want in your corner when it comes to getting things done. She is tenacious and passionate about her beliefs. If she is on your side, you have a fierce ally who is ready and willing to stand up for you. She looks out for me, but she knows how to have a good time as well. She's just usually trying to make sure Hailee, Daniel and I are where we need to be. Whitney loves reading, studying and learning about the Bible through podcasts and her "She Reads Truth" studies. She tells a great story and will share all the details with an enthusiasm that in itself is entertaining. When the Backstreet Boys, N'Sync, or George Strait come on the radio, you are in for a treat. At home she is usually getting chores done listening to a sermon or singing worship tunes. Her eyes are my favorite color green, and we hate to be apart from one another. The kids can't wait for her to cuddle up with them and read a Bible story. She's the Christian I hope to be one day. Whitney is my favorite person, and we love working together at Riverside Christian Academy.

Cancer

I received the news that my favorite person, my other half, my beloved husband had leukemia on October 16,

2018. Travis is the person who knows me best. He is the person I trust above anyone else, the person who has my back, who never fails to smile when I walk into a room, who shares all my inside jokes. He is the first person I want to tell when something incredible happens. The one who makes my coffee every morning and kisses me before bed each night. At the time of his diagnosis, Travis and I had been married for ten-and-a-half years. We had lived a lot of life together. Most people who know us have a difficult time thinking of one of us without the other; we truly enjoy each other's company that much.

Have you ever thought about what it would be like to hear your favorite person in the world has cancer? If you've never had to experience it, I hope you never have to. It's gut-wrenching. But chances are you will. The National Cancer Institute reported that 1.8 million Americans were diagnosed with cancer in 2019.[1] Imagine the ripple effect of that 1.8 million; cancer doesn't just affect the person who is diagnosed, it affects the whole family, and on many different levels. Cancer isn't just a physical battle against disease, it is a spiritual battle, and an emotional battle that takes a toll on everyone near the patient and lasts for much longer than the duration of treatment.

Cancer is terrible. I hate hearing that someone else I know has been diagnosed with the disease, but I also know that they will see God's hand in their lives in ways they could never have expected before. This story is a chapter from our life's journey. It is a story of suffering and joy; a story of mourning and dancing.

Foster Care/Adoption:

The decision to be a foster parent is a deeply personal and sacrificial one. Like most decisions of this magnitude, you really don't know the depth of such sacrifice until you are in over your head. In the moments you are struggling to catch your breath you realize the importance of those around you. The idea of hospitality to a stranger is a running theme throughout Scripture. From the very beginning of the Bible strangers are given a high priority to receive the greatest of hospitality. There is no greater example of this principle than Jesus' hospitality to all who made the choice to be estranged from him. As Christians we have made the choice to be adopted into God's family, though His offer is open to all. We show our love for God by showing our love and hospitality to everyone around us—at least that is the goal. Hebrews 13:2 (ESV) encourages us "to show hospitality to strangers, for thereby some have entertained angels unawares." I'm not sure I would describe the little strangers who entered our home in 2017 as angelic (although some would) but they sure taught me a thing or two about hospitality and sacrifice.

In the 2020 fiscal year, 631,832 children were served by the foster care system in the United States. Over 200,000 of those entered the system for the first time in 2020. The same study said that 99% of those were from a combination of neglect and drug abuse.[2] The goal of most foster care situations is to reunite the children with their biological parents. The foster parents are seen as mentors not only for the underage but their parents as well. This can be a difficult responsibility to balance and to keep in perspective. In many cases, there is a legacy of abuse and several generations spent in and out of foster homes. Foster parents are tasked with breaking the cycle while also providing a nurturing environment for the kids in their care.

ENDNOTES

[1] American Cancer Society. "Cancer Facts & Figures 2019." Accessed February 14, 2022. https://www.cancer.org/research/cancer-facts-statistics/all-cancer-facts-figures/cancer-facts-figures-2019.html.

[2] Administration for Children and Families, "The AFCARS Report," Accessed February 8, 2022. https://www.acf.hhs.gov/sites/default/files/documents/cb/afcarsreport28.pdf.

CHAPTER 2

A Knight's Tale

T he year before we got married in the fall of 2007, Travis took a job teaching Bible and coaching football at Riverside Christian Academy in Fayetteville, Tennessee. I joined him there in 2008 after we got married. RCA has been our second home and second family ever since. It has been a huge blessing to do daily life and ministry in one place for the last 14 years. We have watched kids grow from Kindergartners to high school graduates and have been blessed to be a part of their lives and their coming to know Jesus. And the best part about all of it is that we get to do it together every day.

***

When I first took the job at Riverside my official title was Campus Minister, Middle and High School Bible teacher, and assistant football coach to Chris Jones. I had coached running backs for Coach Jones at Douglas High School in Northeast Alabama while working as the Youth Minister at

North Broad church of Christ in Albertville. When Coach left Douglas, I stopped coaching until he helped hire me at RCA in 2007. In 2007, RCA was starting its first or second year of eleven-man football. The first game I coached at RCA was actually a middle school game against Fayetteville Middle School. Their mascot is the Tiger and at the time they were using Auburn University's tiger eyes logo. At some point during the game after they scored, they played the unofficial fight song of the University of Tennessee's "Rocky Top" through the PA system. I thought to myself, "What have I gotten myself into, these people are mixing Auburn and Tennessee!" Of course, as an Alabama fan I have my issues with Auburn, but I have an unhealthy aversion to "that team from Knoxville."

My students often have a hard time understanding my disdain of the Volunteers because they haven't beaten Alabama in football since 2006. My dislike for "Big Orange" goes back to my time at Freed-Hardeman University when Tennessee was fresh off a national championship. During my days at FHU the Vols beat Bama most of the time. So anytime Alabama lost, my Orange clad "friends" at FHU would find a way into my room and hide my Alabama gear all over the dorm. Sometimes they would even replace the crimson with the orange. I'm still working out their forgiveness for such crimes, but I don't foresee it coming.

We played eleven-man football at RCA until 2012 when we switched to eight-man football and rejoined the Middle Tennessee Athletic Conference. I was the Offensive Coordinator under Head Coach Daniel Beard. Although the move started out rocky; first we played the defending 8-Man National Champions, the Christian Community School Colts, and the following week the defending Alabama State Cham-

pions. Both teams beat us badly and had us questioning the move. The third week we were able to secure our first victory of the season. From there we got on a roll and went on to win the 2012 Division 2 Conference Championship. Division 2 was for teams with a roster of 25 or less although the smaller teams could play for Division 1 if their record was good enough. I took over as head coach in 2013 and our talent was able to overcome my rookie mistakes to enter the Division 2 championship game with eight wins and two losses. We carried the school's best record in Varsity football into our second game against our rivals, the Franklin Christian Academy Falcons, for the title.

The first time we played the Falcons it was a score fest with their passing attack setting records through the air, but we outlasted them 74-54. Our quarterback Senior Joshua Brooks just refused to lose and had plenty of help from Junior Seth Finch who scored over 20 points in the first game. Unfortunately, Seth along with Senior running back Austin Wooten were both out for the championship game. Going into the game, we had practiced heavily depending on their magnificent passing game. We had also focused on breaking our own offensive tendencies. I hardly ate or slept all week in preparation. To say I was nervous was an understatement.

Apparently, we prepared pretty well for one another because it was scoreless at the end of the first quarter. If you know anything about eight-man football, you know that is rare. It is like arena football but played on a regular size field which allows for the point totals to be high as mentioned earlier. We didn't score many more points in the second quarter with both teams sitting below twenty at the break. The scoring picked up in a hurry after halftime. As the clock ticked *down just below two minutes left in the game, FCA was leading 52-48. We had a nice return following FCA's last score that got us around their fifty-yard line. After a running play my coaching sixth sense said, "It's time." It was time to run the trick play we'd practiced every practice since late July. On this chilly, nerve-wracking November Saturday, it was time. It's the most assured play call I'd ever make. The players had begged and begged to run the play earlier in the season, but every time I denied their request. They were shocked when the play call came in, but they were excited. Now we had to execute. The deceptive "Halfback Toss Pass" was a play that my best friend and first cousin, Ben Hayes, and I had run in video games and in the backyard for 20 years. Alas, I was not playing in 2013, but I had no doubt it would work. Joshua Brooks (the best player on the field) would backward toss the ball to our 260-pound halfback Josh Hill in the play. Everyone (as you might imagine) on the opposing team would run up to try and tackle him because everything they saw was evidence of a running play. The left-handed halfback would surprisingly stop and throw it over their heads to our wide receiver Mason Forchetti who would run into the end-zone. It went exactly as planned! I was stunned that it worked. Our sideline exploded with excitement as did the purple and gold-clad RCA fans. During the celebration, my defensive coordinator Paul Sain walked slowly to my side and pointed to the scoreboard, which now read that we were leading but with almost 2 minutes left to play. Our opponent had a quick-strike offense and could wipe away our lead in seconds if the conditions were right. He respectfully went back to doing his job, attempting to help us hang onto the lead we had just acquired. FCA was able to move the ball down past our thirty-yard line when the quar-*

terback was tackled with ten seconds left and the officials were not able to get the ball spotted in time. It was official! RCA was back-to-back MTAC D2 Conference Champions! I believe that team is still Whitney's favorite.

In 2014, I got way too relaxed and then the injury bug struck, and our season wasn't what it could've been. In 2015, we were able to win our third championship game, renamed at that point the MTAC Bowl. We finished 7-3 and defeated The Webb School in Bell Buckle for the title. In 2016, we would finish with a 7-3 record again but this time we would end the season losing to Christian Community in the MTAC Bowl. 2017 I had my worst record as head coach as we completed the season with one win and nine losses. 2018 would turn out to be the most difficult year in my coaching career.

CHAPTER 3

A New Notion

I turned 30-years-old in the fall of 2016. I was suddenly overwhelmed at the thought that I had spent three decades on this earth, and I didn't feel like I was having an impact on the world for Christ. Everyone I interacted with in my day-to-day life either already had a personal relationship with Jesus or had every access to choose Him. I never had interactions with people who didn't know Jesus or have the chance to know Him. I had a deep feeling in my bones that this had to change. I just wasn't sure how I was going to add more to my plate. I knew that this ministry would have to be something I could fit into my life as I was going and doing life and ministry through RCA and my church.

Foster parenting dropped into my mind while I was out on a run one hot September afternoon. I was running down a long hill close to my house. Both sides of the road have large trees that form a shady canopy. When I had that thought, I stopped running, and started walking; I even asked myself, *where did that come from?* I've never wanted to be a foster parent. In fact, I remember saying many times that I would adopt if that was in God's plan for me, but I never wanted to foster—insert eye roll. I've just tried to stop using the words always and never when it comes to God's plans for my life. I've figured out He usually just laughs at them, and it's best that I just hold my hands open and say, "Help me to have a desire to do your will."

I thought about the foster parenting thing some more, and prayed about it every few days. And God just kept confirming. It started with my friend Britney talking about how we had the perfect set-up to be a good foster family for some children, from our home to our school and church family. Then I started seeing signs. I mean *literal* campaign signs. There were foster parent recruitment signs everywhere I went...the bank, Dollar General, CVS. After that, came the messages, *literal radio messages.* Nick Saban, the University of Alabama's Head Football Coach, was recruiting foster parents on ads placed during the Tide's games. I worked up the courage about a month later to mention it to Travis. By this time, God had worked on my heart and I was ready. Travis on the other hand was not ready yet.

Then one Sunday night, God confirmed all the nudges, signs, and messages I had been experiencing in a shocking and unexpected way. Our friends Britney and Josh invited us to their church for a monthly worship night, so we made the 40 minute drive south to Huntsville to meet up with them. We all enjoyed burgers and sweet potato fries at Farm Burger, our favorite grass-fed burger joint, before driving across the road to their church for the worship service. Most of the people in the building were standing and singing, including myself, when Britney sat down for a minute or two before tugging on the sleeve of my Chicago Bears sweat jacket. I sat down next to her, and she looked at me intently and asked a question that I wasn't expecting.

"Are you pregnant?" she asked.

"No," I replied, with confusion.

"Are you sure?"

"Yes, I'm very sure."

Then she spoke the words that confirmed all the conversations I had been having with the Lord. She said, "Well I just saw an image of an ultrasound while we were worshipping, and God said that he is preparing you to be a mother."

I hadn't told anyone but Travis what the Lord was saying. Those words echoed in my mind as a reminder repeatedly over the next several months and years when the fostering journey seemed to be more than I could handle. Those words still comfort me when I feel like I'm failing in the parenting department; I remember that God prepared me for the good works he had planned for me to do (Ephesians 2:10).

***

God had been working on my heart, too. I had heard the Nick Saban commercials several times. I'd also known several couples growing up who had been foster parents, especially some of my cousins on my mother's side of the family. In particular, Doug and Linda Hayes, who had been foster parents for several children throughout the years. Also, Kirk and Andrea Hayes had adopted their son, so I wasn't a stranger to the idea. My misgivings were because foster care promotes the successful return of the kids to their biological parents. I knew "giving them back" would be gut-wrenching.

On a trip to Tuscaloosa, my dear friend and Special Teams Coordinator/Defensive Backs Coach Kevin Whitworth mentioned that he believed Whitney and I would provide a good home for foster care. That meant a lot coming from Coach as he had an adopted son, Marcus. If we could pour into some kids and see them become half the young man Marcus is, what a blessing that would be! Coach's encouragement really started the wheels turning. Less than two weeks later, Whitney brought it up again. Although we had talked about adopting a child from a foreign country in passing, I could tell Whitney was serious. I mentioned my hesitation but said I would think and pray on it some more.

A week or so later it was the "Third Saturday in October", the annual rivalry game between Alabama and that "team from Knoxville." I try to find something else to do during that game, so instead, I drove down to Huntsville to conduct some research at Barnes and Noble. I looked at a few books that only reassured me of the pitfalls, but I was reminded of all the preaching and teaching I had done on Scriptures that tell us to trust God and love him by loving others. I had poked fun at Jonah countless times for running from God. How ridiculous was it to run from a God who is everywhere? There I was in my hamster wheel trying every way to ignore what I knew I should do.

***

By Thanksgiving, Travis was on board for the foster parent certification classes! We registered with the Tennessee Department of Children's Services for PATH (Parents as Tender Healers) Classes to begin the first week of December. Every Thursday night for the months of December and January, we loaded up in my black Toyota Tundra and made the hour-long drive down TN-Hwy 64 to Lawrenceburg. The classes were hosted in an old antebellum-style house that had once served as a children's home. The building was being used as a clothing closet at the time. They offered free new and gently used clothes, baby gear, and children's items to licensed foster families and children in need. There was a large dining area with a fireplace to the right of the foyer entrance. The area was filled with long, white, plastic tables and folding chairs, and there was a projector screen at the front of the room. Over the next eight weeks we learned everything from how to navigate the child welfare system, to the effects of trauma, to CPR.

The classes lasted for 3-4 hours each week, so we were pretty tired by the time we drove home, but we found the energy to chat about all that we had learned. I feel like the classes were very informative and provided information and tools for prospective foster parents in the best way possible, but there is just nothing that can *really* prepare you for what it will be like the first time DCS drops a couple of kids off at your door. "The knowing" and "the doing" are two different things. I guess it's kind of like premarital counseling. It's important to have the knowledge and tools counseling provides but putting those things into action day in and day out in a relationship is tough work.

We went through the process of certification classes, interviews, and the home study. I put out a plea for baby/kid gear and furniture on Facebook sometime in January. The post said:

> Hey friends...Travis and I are in the process of becoming licensed foster parents. We have almost completed training and will begin the home study process soon. We need some items to complete the home study process...if you have any of the following items and need them taken off your hands, please send me a price and a pic: baby crib, car seat (preferably one that will convert from infant to a larger child), twin bed, and/or a dresser. We would also like to ask for your prayers as we start this journey :)

Within a couple of days there were over 200 likes on the post and over 50 comments from people offering us the items we needed to pass the home study, and their love, support, and prayers. Within a week we had everything we needed to pass the home study and more. A parent from our school contacted me with loads of baby items that we needed. God knew exactly what was coming because the Gibson's were cleaning out their twins' baby items. They had two of almost everything we needed. I thanked everyone for their offers on Facebook and let them know that we found everything at a one-stop shop called the Gibson home. They gave us everything from car seats, a rocking chair, blocks (these are still my son's favorite toys), books, puzzles, child-size plates and cups, bedding, and a baby bed. Our home study writer said that our process was moving at record pace, and that she was so impressed with the community of support around us. It was such a blessing to see all the people who love and support us. We were fully certified by March of 2017. We waited eagerly for our first placement call to come. By that time, we were both excited about welcoming a child into our home.

CHAPTER 4

Hailee & Daniel

T
he first call came on Wednesday, April 12. I spoke to a DCS case manager around 5:30 that evening. She asked if we would take an 11-year-old boy from a neighboring county. I was at home alone cooking a dish for church that night, and Travis was driving the church van to pick up some teenagers who needed a ride to worship. I asked if I could call her back in about 30 minutes after talking to Travis. She said that would be fine, but they were going to take him to a nearby foster home for temporary placement for the night since it was already getting late. She said she would begin looking for permanent placement again in the morning, and that we would talk again the next day about bringing the boy to our house if Travis and I were still interested.

Travis and I talked and prayed about our answer, and we decided to accept the placement the next morning. I remember telling the teenagers in my Bible class at school that we may have our first foster care placement by the end of the day. The girls were very excited. They had been praying for us through the whole process. They asked if I would bring the child to spring formal that night so they could meet him. I told them I wasn't sure yet; and that it would all depend on if he felt like going.

I was excited and nervous as I picked up my cell phone to call the case manager back soon after the DCS offices opened that morning. As I dialed, I prayed, "Lord your will be done." I told the case manager that Travis and I were ready to accept the boy as our first placement, and we were excited about welcoming him into our home. She was very thankful and said she would give me a call back to arrange a time to bring him over.

Again, I was excited and nervous. I walked down the steps from my second-floor classroom to my first-floor office. My phone rang, and when I answered the DCS case manager on the other end of the line said, "Mrs. Creasy, I just talked to the foster parents in the temporary home that we placed the young man in last night, and they want to keep him."

"Don't be sorry!" I said quickly. "I'm so glad that he is in a good home where he is thriving."

"They said he was doing great, and they love him, and he fits in their family very well. I'm so sorry."

I replied, "I know it is hard to find the right fit. It's a blessing for him that it happened this way."

I had a knowing deep in my gut that God had his hand on the situation. I felt certain that he had a plan I didn't know anything about, and that I just needed to trust and obey. She thanked me for understanding, and said she was sure we would get another placement call soon. She was right.

The second placement call came after four days. Late on

Sunday, April 16, Easter Sunday. I was already in bed for the night. As I laid there reading, my cell phone rang on the nightstand next to me. I reached over, picked up the phone and looked at the caller number. It was a number I didn't recognize, and I immediately thought that it may be another placement call. When I answered, the man on the other the line introduced himself as a DCS placement worker. He sounded tired, like he had been working for hours. He told me they had taken a sibling set into custody in a neighboring county, a one-year-old boy and two-year-old girl. He said they needed a long-term foster home as both parents would need to work a parenting plan to regain their custody. He asked if we would be interested in taking them. I asked him if I could talk to my husband, and give him a call back in a few minutes, and he said that would be fine.

I walked downstairs to find Travis in the "man cave," our multi-purpose basement room that housed all the Alabama football memorabilia, my spin bike, and Travis' gaming systems. I told him that DCS had just called, and they wanted to know if we would take a one-year-old boy and two-year-old girl.

He asked, "Do we even have two baby beds?"

I said, "No, but one of them could sleep in the baby bed in the upstairs bedroom, and the other could sleep in the pack-and-play for a few days until we could find another baby bed.

"We should say yes." He said, "This has been prayed over for a long time by a lot of people."

I called the placement manager back and told him we would take both kids. He sounded so relieved and grateful. He said the case manager on call and a child protective services worker would be bringing them to our home as soon as possible.

The next person I called was my mom. I remember telling her we had accepted our first foster care placement, and that they would be there soon.

"Wow! They?" She asked.

I told her about them.

She immediately said, "Oh Whitney what have you done?"

"I don't know, mom? What have I done?" Was the only thing I could think to say. I had never been a parent. I had never raised kids. I was completely ignorant as to what it took to raise children. Which in some ways, I think is a good thing. I would not have had the guts to say yes to this calling from God if I had truly understood what it entailed, but I believe God doesn't necessarily call the qualified; I know he qualifies those he calls.

"You're young, you'll be fine. It's going to take a lot of energy though. Those are little babies."

I immediately said, "Well, I guess I better let you go and see what I can get done to prepare before they get here."

Travis and I set our minds to figuring out how to get the pack-and-play ready for one of the babies to sleep in. YouTube was a Godsend! We had never even opened the pack-and-play that had been given to us by one of the church members. We got it out and unrolled the Winnie the Pooh mat that went in the bottom of the pack-and-play for the baby to sleep on and just looked at each other like, "what do we do with this thing?" I'm pretty sure we both said, "YouTube" at the same time—there are YouTube tutorials for everything.

Once we got the pack-and-play set up, we moved outside to install the car seats. We were armed with a flashlight and cell phone so we could watch the YouTube tutorials for car seat installation. While we were fighting the car seats in the dark driveway, the Child Protective Services worker called my phone.

He said, "Mrs. Creasy,"

I answered, "yes" very quickly.

"I have Hailee and Daniel," he said. It was the first time I heard their names. I hadn't even asked the DCS placement worker what their names were.

The CPS worker continued, "We are leaving the hospital, and we have to stop to get the paperwork at the DCS office, then we will make our way to your house."

I quickly thought through their estimated time of arrival, and realized we had some time to make it to Walmart to pick up some essentials. So, I said, "Ok we will be ready when you get here." Then I asked if he knew if the children had any clothes or diapers.

He said, "They don't have much of anything, just a plastic bag with a few items in it."

When I hung up the phone, I told Travis I was going in to get my purse because we had time to go to Walmart. On the way, Travis called his cousin Ben to ask what foods his five kids ate. He had a few suggestions as we pulled into the parking lot. We wandered up and down the aisles of Walmart picking up everything we thought we may need. We bought cheerios, apple sauce, bananas, eggs, milk, apple juice, diapers, and wipes.

We wandered to the children's clothes section and decided to buy each child a couple of pairs of pajamas. We had to guess at sizes because we didn't actually know how big they were; we only knew their ages. Travis had picked up a pair of little boy's pajamas in an 18 months size. I thought they were cute, and we put them in the cart, but then I stumbled across a pair of blue and white striped pajamas with a lion on the chest. I picked them up and said, "No, Daniel needs these pajamas!" I thought about the story of Daniel in the Lion's Den in the Bible.

Travis just looked at me a little dumbfounded, and said, "His name is Daniel?" I realized I never told Travis their names! I was too busy thinking about what all we needed to buy when I got off the phone with the CPS worker.

I said, "Yes, his name is Daniel."

Then Travis asked, "What is the little girl's name?"

"Hailee."

He repeated their names together, "Hailee and Daniel." He said it kind of slowly, like he was testing out the sound of it coming off his lips.

If you're a fan of the television show The Office, you will remember Jim and Pam's wedding episode. There is a running string throughout the episode, where Jim and Pam make mental photos of the special and quirky moments of their wedding weekend in Niagara Falls by making the shape of a camera with their fingers in front of their face, pretending to press the capture button with their right index finger, and making a clicking noise like they had just taken a snapshot of the moment with an imaginary camera. When Travis repeated Hailee and Daniel's names to himself standing there in the children's pajama section of Walmart at 10:00 p.m., I saw Pam's face flash across my mind as she made a mental snapshot of Jim just before they walked down the aisle. I made a mental snapshot of my husband saying the names of our children for the first time. I didn't know they would be our children one day; I only knew this moment was special, and I would look back on it with more clarity in the future.

We made it home and unloaded our purchases. I'm not sure how long we waited for the CPS worker and the DCS case manager to make it to our house with the kids. It's weird to think back on it now, but I had no idea that I was living the last few moments before I would become a mother. But there I was kind of pacing around my home finding things to keep busy until my babies arrived.

I sent a text to my "office ladies" at RCA. I told them I wouldn't be in the next day because we were getting our first foster care placement. They offered their encouragement and prayers and told me to let them know if they could do anything for me at work.

I tended to my sunburned shoulders that were getting sore after an afternoon of planting vegetables in raised beds. I did some spot-cleaning so the house would look more presentable, that would prove to be futile in the coming days. Cleaning while having a one-year-old and a two-year-old in the house is about like trying to clean up debris during a tornado.

I don't remember who noticed they had pulled in the driveway first. I just remember opening the door to a woman with short, spiky blonde hair, dark red lipstick, and a black jacket with a load of paperwork in one arm and a baby carrier/car seat in the other. A man stood behind her. He was much taller; he towered over her from behind. He spoke a tired greeting and I recognized his voice as the man I spoke with on the phone. He was a middle-aged gentleman with graying hair and his face wore an expression that said he had been beat down by the day's events. But the most noticeable thing about the man was the two-year-old little girl in his arms.

Hailee had her arms wrapped around the man's neck, a baby bottle full of apple juice clutched in one hand, her head laid on his shoulder, and her legs wrapped around his waist. The woman sat the baby carrier down on the floor of my living room. I looked down to see little Daniel for the first time. He was sleeping soundly. His little head was tilted to one side and his lips were pressed together in deep sleep. His blonde hair was thin around the sides with a thick tousle right on top that came to a point on his forehead. He and Hailee both wore little pediatric hospital gowns with zoo animals on them. The man sat down on the loveseat in my living room with Hailee still draped around him. I realized she was asleep because she never moved. Her blonde hair covered her face, so I couldn't see anything about her features.

The woman turned out to be the Head of the Department of Children's Services in the neighboring county. She walked us through the load of paperwork and assured us she was placing one of her best case managers on this case, and that we would hear from her the next day. When all the papers were signed, and all the questions (that we could think of) were asked and answered, it was time for them to leave us there with the children...alone. I remember trying to peel Hailee off the CPS worker, and she immediately began screaming, which woke up Daniel in his baby carrier. The two social workers exited the front door as the sounds of

Hailee's screams drifted out into the front yard in the otherwise still and peaceful night.

I tried to console her, talk to her, offer her snacks, drinks, a toy, and a blanket. This wasn't looking good. Everything I had learned to do when a new placement arrived had failed. The screaming only got louder, and she became more and more enraged the more I tried to help. I still hadn't seen her face, because every time I tried to brush her hair out of her eyes, she just pulled the matted mess back over them again. When she started swinging at me and kicking, I decided it was time to lay her down in the bed with a bottle, a stuffed animal, and a soft blanket. She was so exhausted from all that she endured that day, she was asleep in less than two minutes. Daniel, on the other hand, was wide awake at that point. He cried the rest of the night, other than when Travis took him on a ride in the car, and when he laid down in our bed with him sprawled out on his chest.

I texted my mom around 3:00 a.m. and told her the baby hadn't slept all night. She said she would come help me in the morning. She must have left Albertville on the hour-and-a-half trek as soon as it was daylight because she pulled up in my driveway a little after 7:00 a.m. Hailee was still sound asleep, but Daniel was wide awake for the day. I was sitting in the living room feeding him a GoGo Squeeze packet of applesauce when mom arrived. I had just texted her and my sister Bailey a picture of him sitting on the rug in the living room. He was wearing only a diaper and still had the tape and cotton ball on his arm from where they had drawn his blood at the hospital the night before. When I saw mom's car in the driveway, I picked Daniel up, put him on my hip, and unlocked the front door for her. Her eyes welled with tears at the sight of him. She asked where Hailee was.

I said, "She's still asleep, and we're going to try to keep it that way for a while. I don't know what we will do when she gets up." I was very worried that she would pick up where she had left off the night before.

We gave little Daniel a bath and put him in his new lion pajamas. It was a good thing we had made the whirlwind Walmart run the night before. The CPS worker was right. They didn't have much of anything in their plastic grocery bag. There was a t-shirt for Daniel and a dress for Hailee, neither of which fit. There were about five diapers for the two of them, two dirty sippy cups, and several broken plastic Easter eggs.

I love spring and Easter. I think about those broken plastic eggs every year as the winter begins to warm, and the days begin to get longer; as the daffodils poke their heads out from their long hibernation, and birds can be heard chirping in the morning. It's a time of new beginnings. A time when you can almost feel the ache of the winter darkness being undone, just like Mary Magdalene's mourning at the tomb turned to joy on that resurrection Sunday when she realized the gardener she had been talking to was Jesus, her beloved rescuer.

On that Easter Sunday in 2017, I thought those broken plastic Easter eggs were a small picture of what had happened in the lives of the two small children who were now under my care. Their little world had been splintered. They had been torn apart from everything they had ever known very quickly, and they didn't know or understand why. Their whole world was broken, just like those eggs.

***

It doesn't take much to remind me of that day but when I think of those little plastic Easter eggs it hits me. The items of those Walmart sacks, the memory of those sad little hospital gowns and my little girl clinging to a complete stranger for comfort breaks my heart. They had so little to give; the world had already taken too much from them. The next few days would reveal a lot about me as a person. Those days and the days to come will continue to reveal what little I have to offer God in return for what he did and is doing. In comparison to what he has, my offering is less than the contents of those little Walmart bags. The contents of those meager bags did not make those kids more or less loved. It wasn't about what they brought with them to my house. We wanted them regardless of their belongings or what they had to offer.

I'm reminded of Jesus' statement in Matthew 7:11 (ESV) "If you then, who are evil, know how to give good gifts to your children, how much more will your Father who is in heaven give good things to those who ask him!" The point is that life got harder with these young ones and there were times we didn't know if our house was the best place for them. God is not overwhelmed with you. He wants you and all your Walmart bags of struggle no matter how big. It isn't about what you have to offer. It is about how much he wants you (John 3:16). Those plastic eggs represented a normal day for so many. A normal day for my kids—the full details I may never know. A "normal day" that changed their lives and mine forever.

***

Hailee woke up a little while later, and when I heard her cooing upstairs, I looked nervously at my mom before I moved. I said a prayer as I made my way up the stairs, asking God to help me know how to make her feel loved and safe. When I opened the door, she was standing up in the baby bed, still wearing the hospital gown from the night before. I could finally see her face; she looked a lot like Daniel. Both had blue eyes and round cheeks. She didn't have the look of fear in her eyes that had been there the night before. She seemed to just be taking in the room as she looked around. I had no idea how much she could talk or even if she could understand what I said. I remember saying something like, "Good morning, Hailee. My name is Whitney. This is my house, and I'm so happy that you are here to stay with me for a little while. I have a cat downstairs; do you want to go see it?"

She was very excited about the cat and put her arms in the air and grunted for me to come pick her up. I immediately scooped her up and headed down the steps for her to see the cat before she changed her mind. We found my cat, affectionately known as Kitty Man, perched on the half wall that divides my living room from the kitchen. He welcomed Hailee's attention and acted curious about where these two tiny humans had come from.

It was becoming more and more obvious that Hailee didn't have much more communication ability than Daniel. She had a lot of grunts, oohs, ahs, and other expressions that all had their own meanings, which we picked up on fairly quickly.

Mom made her way over with Daniel, and Hailee excitedly exclaimed, "Bubba!" By the end of the day, we realized her whole inventory of words included: Bubba, momma, no and mine. Those first few days, weeks, and months were very hard for many reasons, but one of the main reasons was that Hailee had so many things she wanted to say, but she had no way to communicate. Her frustration at her lack of ability to communicate and our lack of ability to understand came out in tantrums and fits of rage. I look back on those days now, and my heart hurts for all of us. My heart hurts for Hailee because I'm sure she understood more than we realized, and we had no idea how to answer her questions or even what those questions were.

Doris, my mother-in-law, made her way to our home on Monday afternoon. Daw as the kids began to call her became Daniel's favorite in our household from the first time they met. He snuggled up with her in the rocking chair and hung on to her shirt tightly with his little fist. Doris helped for a few days as we figured out a routine to help the kids feel safe and give them some predictability and stability. She helped with everything from cooking meals to the bedtime routine. Her presence for those first few days was comforting and foundational.

I spent a lot of time on the phone trying to find a daycare that would take both children, but I wasn't having any luck. There were no daycares in the county that had openings for children their age. There was one daycare on the other side of the county that said they would have a spot for the two-year-old in two weeks, but they couldn't promise anything for the baby. If I had realized the difficulty of finding daycare for children that age, I may not have accepted the placement, but God had his hand on the situation once again. He took care of us in ways that were beyond my expectations.

My boss let me take the week off to get the kids acclimated to being in our home, and two friends from church, Debbie and Denise, volunteered to keep the kids while I was at work until we could get them in daycare. The second week the kiddos were in our house, they began staying with Debbie and Denise. We took them to Debbie's house on Mondays and Fridays, and Denise came to our house to stay with them on Tuesdays, Wednesdays, and Thursdays. This was the beginning of our "village." From the old saying, "it takes a village to raise a child." It is *so* true. I am so thankful that God placed a village of people around us to help raise these children. We are blessed beyond measure with people who love our children like their own, who spoil them, and who point them to truth.

After about two weeks, Hailee had a spot in daycare, and about a month after that Daniel got a spot too. The daycare was across the county, so it wasn't very conveniently located, but in the days and weeks that followed we came to understand that these kiddos were in the perfect place.

The first day we took Hailee to daycare, she dove out of my arms and into Mrs. Sharon's arms. Mrs. Sharon was her first teacher at Kingdom Kids Learning Center. Up until that point, she hadn't willingly left me for anyone else. In fact, she had been clinging to my leg and screaming anytime a new person came to our door at home, so her willingness to join Mrs. Sharon in class was surprising and relieving.

The women at Kingdom Kids loved Hailee and Daniel like their own. One day, when I went to pick Daniel up, I found him cuddled up with his teacher Mrs. Ionia. She said,

"I know we have to put him down more or he will never learn to walk, but he's just so cuddly." Mrs. Karen was Hailee's teacher for a short period until she was potty-trained, but she was Daniel's teacher for a long time because he was a stubborn potty-trainer. She was the perfect match for my strong-willed boy. She was a disciplinarian who made him toe the line but would also light up and say his name like he was the most special boy in the world every time she saw him. Mrs. Alicia and Mrs. Glenda were a mother-daughter duo that taught the two oldest classrooms of children, and they made each child feel special and loved.

Then there was Mrs. Doris or DahDah as the kids (and parents) called her. She loved every child that walked through the doors of that daycare. She called them all by name. She kissed every one of them goodbye in the afternoon. She toted them around on her hip or sometimes under her arm like a sack of potatoes. She never forgets anyone either. Just a few months ago, she was driving by our house and saw us out in the yard playing. She had her husband pull over, just so she could get out and love on the kids and talk to us. The daycare was the ministry of a local church, so the children learned Bible stories, hymns, and said prayers every day. We loved "Baby School" as the kids call it now. These people were a part of our village too.

The first few months of foster care were just *tough*. Going from a family of two to a family of four with two babies who relied on us for everything was more difficult than I anticipated. The weekends were especially tough. It seemed like by the time we reached Sunday afternoon everyone's nerves were shot. We used to plan an outing to make the time between nap time and bedtime seem shorter in those early days. One weekend we went to eat dinner at a Chick-fil-A on Whitesburg Drive in Huntsville. The restaurant had a play area at the time, so we ate dinner and let Hailee play while we entertained Daniel with some toys at the picnic tables outside.

Another couple was there with two children about the same ages as Hailee and Daniel. They were kind and made conversation with us for a while. The dad said, "Going from one to two kids felt more like going from one to four kids, didn't it?"

Travis and I looked at each and shrugged, then I looked back at him and said, "We wouldn't know." He seemed confused, because Hailee and Daniel obviously weren't twins, so I explained further. "We went from none to two. These kids came to us a couple of months ago through the Department of Children's Services. We're fostering them."

The man's mouth opened a little bit, and then he said, "Wow, would it be ok if we asked our church family to pray for you?"

I said, "Please do, we could use all the prayers we can get!"

For months, possibly over a year, I would blast Lauren Daigle's *How Can It Be* album as we made the drive from our house to the daycare every day. I would sing the song "O Lord" at the top of my lungs! The lyrics spoke to me and pointed me to the one place where hope could be found in that season of life, and in all seasons of life.

> Though times it seems
> Like I'm coming undone
> This walk can often feel lonely

No matter what until this race is won
I will stand my ground where hope can be found
I will stand my ground where hope can be found
Oh, O' Lord, O' Lord, I know You hear my cry
Your love is lifting me above all the lies
No matter what I face this I know in time
You'll take all that is wrong and make it right
You'll take all that is wrong and make it right
Your strength is found
At the end of my road
Your grace it reaches to the hurting
Still through the tears and the questioning why
I will stand my ground where hope can be found
I will stand my ground where hope can be found[1]

I would belt this song with the kids squabbling in the backseat; I was thinking about how my own life seemed to be coming undone amid their trauma, about how I seemed to be failing at every turn, about how I didn't know how I could keep going with all of it on my shoulders, about how I probably made a mistake, and that I had taken on more than I could handle. But Lauren's words would echo, "I will stand my ground where hope can be found." That line reminded me of what was true, and that there was only one place where I could find hope, and that was in Jesus.

ENDNOTES

[1] Daigle, Lauren. "Oh Lord." Track #2 How Can It Be. Centricity Music, 2015, Compact Disc.

CHAPTER 5

A Season of Transformation

The summer of 2017 crept slowly by, but by the time September came things were a lot easier. We had been parenting for 5 months, and we had found a groove in our daily schedule. The kids were growing and learning and developing attachments to us and their village of people who helped us raise them. They were slowly learning there were a lot of loving, kind, and trustworthy people in their world now. It took a long time for Hailee to trust anyone other than myself. In fact, I used to ask anyone who was coming to our house to send me a picture of themselves and bring her something...anything...a balloon, a sucker, some bubbles. I would show her the picture, and tell her the person's name, how we knew them, and why they were coming to visit. After months and months of introducing the kids to our friends and family and helping them build trust with the people around them, I saw it all pay off suddenly one September evening in a church parking lot downtown. I remember the moment like it happened yesterday because it gave me a glimpse into what Hailee's personality was like underneath the fear and pain the trauma had caused.

One Fall afternoon, I was scrolling through my Instagram feed when I saw Jimmy Wayne, a country musician that I had enjoyed listening to in my teenage years, standing in front of a restaurant in my hometown of Fayetteville, Tennessee. The caption said he was in town to perform a benefit concert for the local child advocacy center. The event would feature many of his popular songs and stories from his autobiography, *Walk to Beautiful*, which I had just finished reading over the summer. Jimmy has one of the most powerful stories I have ever heard. If you have never read his book, maybe you should put this one down and go buy his. His story is about triumph amid the worst circumstances, giving and receiving unmerited grace, living with gratitude, and paying it forward. It is challenging and inspiring.

So, when I saw this Instagram post, I immediately set out to find tickets to the show. Luckily there were tickets still available on the event's website. I purchased one ticket for me and one for Hailee. I thought it would be a good girls' night out for the two of us, and a good opportunity for Travis and Daniel to spend time together at home. So, when Travis made it home from football practice, Hailee and I loaded up in the car and headed downtown to First Methodist Church. I had dressed her in a red, white, and blue dress with a matching red bow in her hair. When I parked the car and went around to the side to unbuckle her from the car seat, another car pulled in and parked next to us. An older woman with short gray hair and glasses climbed out of the car at the same time Hailee and I were making our way toward the church.

The woman smiled at us and said to Hailee, "What a beautiful dress you're wearing!" Hailee immediately looked up at me, and then back at the woman. She let go of my hand and skipped over to her and hugged her around her blue-jean-clad legs. I'm sure my chin hit the asphalt! I was so shocked! Nowadays, this kind of behavior would not be shocking at all from my sweet and loving girl. Just last quarter, her teacher, Mrs. Alford, selected her for the "Fruit of the Spirit Award." I was one proud momma because Mrs. Alford said she had a difficult time choosing if Hailee's Fruit of the Spirit Award would be for love or joy because she embodied both.

As the days went by, our love for these two kiddos who were dropped on our doorstep on Easter Sunday grew exponentially. Our biological families and our church family spoiled them and showered them with love, affection, and prayers. They fit in their little "village" like they were always meant to be there.

***

My reluctance to become a foster parent had a lot to do with the fact that the end goal was to reunite them with their biological parents. You get attached and then you get your heart ripped out, then you are expected to start all over again. I realize now that fear has much to do with my own trust issues. Because my parents divorced when I was a child, I had made a commitment to be the best dad possible. My dad and I for whatever reason don't have a very committed relationship. We don't communicate on a regular basis. I text on Father's Day and when big events happen in my life. I've forgiven him but it is such a habit now that I don't even really think about reaching out.

Due to the nature of our relationship, I have always been hungry for belonging and loyalty. I see the draw of gangs to kids without a parent, especially without a dad in the home. I was surrounded by big families on both sides that took an interest in my wellbeing. My church did the same so I know what being intentional looks like. I have my own village of people who kept me alive. Of course, some of them couldn't get away from me even if they wanted to, I'm thinking of you, Ben Hayes, and my "double-first cousins." Yes, my family tree could probably stand a few more forks but it worked out as I was surrounded by a village of people who at the very least had patience and at best loved me unconditionally. I'm sure folks had their hands full with me even if they didn't let on about it. I'll never be able to repay the blessing of so many who helped my single mom raise three boys, one of which had cerebral palsy.

I believe these "clouds of witnesses" are the reason I've spent most of my life in an official ministry role. I say "official" because I believe all Christians are ministers. I first heard the phrase "Be where your feet are" from motivational speaker Kevin Elko. It makes a lot of Bible sense, but it also applies in a secular way. You can have a tremendous amount of influence if you are aware of your surroundings. There are always people to help who are struggling. Because all people struggle, we will never run out of good things to do. My definition of righteousness is not the question of "Have I done enough to qualify?" but "How can I help further?"

As a Christian, I believe consistent righteousness can only be accomplished through the work of God's Holy Spirit dwelling in us. For that reason, I've spent my life in ministry. I want to draw young people to the LORD. God is a multiplier so he can take our meager (in comparison to His power) offerings of consistency and a genuine heart and compound them to His glory. I remember being taught the stories of the "heroes" of the Old Testament and being awed by their amazing feats. As I got older, I began to realize it wasn't necessarily their greatness but God's that accomplished those great feats. Many of them were downright scoundrels but God remained consistent. He not only overcame their failings but allowed them to thrive despite them. That has encouraged me greatly. I want to give God my best, but regardless, he triumphs. Guys, I understood that with my brain!

Now that I'm a foster parent, I have a vivid flesh and blood understanding of the "triumphant God" concept. I thought I was unselfish. I thought I was pretty solid at serving. Then these two babies showed up on my doorstep. I got a living, breathing reminder of just how selfish I was. Turns out that I really liked having free time, bingeing television shows and not having plans on Saturday. We went from having those things to not having them. I know that a "normal" situation with kids involves sacrificing those things as well. Just add meetings with the kid's representative, your representative, the CASA worker, required dentist/doctor appointments, visitation with parents, and the court dates. In our experience, the court dates involved waiting for an hour or so just to have the judge lay eyes on the kids for five minutes, ask a few questions and send you on your merry way.

There were times when I prayed for their parents to get

their lives right so Hailee and Daniel could go home. Then there were times I begged God not to let them go. I can remember a particular time when Daniel was refusing to go to sleep and nothing I did seemed to matter. I began singing the song "With Christ As My Vessel" that I had sung hundreds of times at camp, CYC and Vacation Bible School. I soon realized I wasn't singing it to soothe him but to soothe myself. On those late nights, I'd sometimes look at that baby boy and tell God "I can't do this!" On that particular night whether it was my own lack of sleep or actually the LORD I don't know, but I heard the message in reply from the back of my mind "I know but I can." I'd like to say from then on, I was sold out. That would be a lie. It certainly helped, and I've hung onto those words ever since, but I had no idea at that moment just how much those words would mean to me.

Eventually the tide would turn, and my prayers would change to wanting the biological parents to get their life right but for God to make a way that we could still be a part of Hailee and Daniel's life. Whitney and I decided to do our due diligence in the avenues that were available, we helped not only Hailee and Daniel, but their parents as well. Once again, I was somewhat dragging my feet in regard to their parents. You may think God is using you to make an impact but he's also impacting you. My poor attitude said more about me and my maturity than anyone else. My idea of "deserving" and "worthy" has been transformed. That transformation has been a tremendous blessing. The transformation continues and I'm reminded once again that anything worth doing is going to have its difficult moments.

CHAPTER 6

Parents' Weekend Out

In October of 2018, Travis and I had been parenting non-stop with very few breaks to reconnect as husband and wife. Life had been stressful with the addition of our two kiddos. We faced several challenges with the new arrivals, so needless to say after 18 months of caring for them, we needed a getaway to spend some time together, just the two of us. So, we planned a trip to Nashville for the weekend, which is a quick drive just 70 miles north on I-65 from our home in Lincoln County. We had plans to stay in a hotel and spend the weekend watching football, eating good food, sleeping late, having uninterrupted conversations, and just being together.

As we prepared for our weekend getaway to Nashville, Travis decided to contact Vanderbilt University. The Commodores are generous to give high school football coaches complimentary tickets to their games. We were in luck, Vandy was facing off against their SEC East rivals the Florida Gators, and there were tickets left. Travis reserved our tickets for the Vanderbilt vs. Florida game on Saturday, and I had already purchased Travis some tickets to the Tennessee Titans vs. Baltimore Ravens game on Sunday. We both just love the sport, so we follow several NFL teams, but the Ravens are Travis' favorite team. He had never seen them play live, so when I saw they were playing in Nashville during our getaway I knew we couldn't miss the opportunity.

We started our much-needed weekend of reconnection with a relaxing couples massage and shopping when we got to town on Friday. We checked into our hotel that afternoon and went up to get unloaded and cleaned up before going out for a nice dinner. The hotel was beautiful with high ceilings, swanky mid-century modern furnishings, and warm fireplaces throughout. Everything seemed perfect until Travis started changing clothes for dinner.

We noticed he was bruised all over his body where the massage therapist had touched him. I was perplexed; I wasn't bruised. I wondered if his therapist had just worked on him too hard. He had already had one big black bruise show up on his side less than two weeks prior that looked like someone had colored on him with a big fat black Sharpie marker.

He hadn't even realized it was there. I just noticed it when he took his shirt off to change clothes after football practice one day. We assumed it was due to the combination of two medications he had been taking for back pain because the side effects of both medications were bruising. I had a gnawing feeling in my gut about the whole thing, but Travis didn't seem to be very worried about it, and he was anxious to spend our weekend together having fun, after all he is the one who never wants to miss out on a party!

We spent Saturday watching collegiate Southeastern football at Vanderbilt Stadium. It was a cold, windy day in Nashville on that Saturday, and everything just looked gray. It was the first time we had been to a college football game since the kids had come to live with us, so we were giddy to spend the day together enjoying our favorite sport. We took a selfie together and I posted it to Instagram with the caption, "We're Vandy fans today, go 'Dores!"

We both enjoyed the game immensely, even though Vanderbilt ended up losing, the atmosphere was fun. I can remember Travis commenting several times during the game that he just could not get warm. I didn't think a lot of it at the time because it was a cold, damp, windy day, and it was the first real cold snap we had in Tennessee that fall, so no one was quite used to the abrupt drop in temperature. Everyone was bundled up in their black and gold hoodies, coats, and hats to protect themselves from the early onset of cold temperatures.

Following the game, we met our friend Tori for dinner and a special treat of ice cream at Nashville's famous "Jennie's Ice Cream." The ice cream shop smelled sweet and was brightly lit and painted white, so it was a nice contrast to the cold, gray day outside. The freezer case had tons of flavor options. Tori and I settled on a dairy-free fruit sorbet while Travis went with something more classic like chocolate. We sat down to continue our evening's conversation, but Travis didn't seem as interested in his treat as we were. In fact, I noticed that he didn't eat much of his ice cream at all. When we left the ice cream shop the majority of it along with the waffle cone went in the trash can; skipping out on a sweet or dessert is very atypical for Travis. He's very much a "treat-yo-self" kind of guy, especially when on vacation or when there is a reason to celebrate. He would have been able to keep up with the characters Donna Meagle and Tom Haverford from NBC's Parks & Rec on their annual "Treat Yo Self Day" with no problem. I was perplexed at his lack of interest in his ice cream, but I didn't think about it too much.

We went to watch the Alabama game at Tori's apartment, then went back to the hotel. The weekend had started off great, but something was different when I awoke on Sunday morning. Something was wrong. I couldn't lay a finger on it. Was it the kids at home? They were being cared for by my mother-in-law Doris and her sister Edith. There weren't any messages or texts from them, but I called just to check in. All was well. Travis and I continued to have emotional turmoil over what the future held for them. We loved them so much and had raised them for so long from such young ages that we ached at the thought of them returning home, but at the time it looked like that was the direction in which things were headed. Maybe that was it. Maybe my morning angst was just the pent-up stress revolving around their littles lives that had become so important to us. I tried not to worry, but for the remainder of the morning I couldn't shake the feeling that something was terribly wrong. Something life changing was brewing amongst us.

***

I always felt weird taking a day off during football season. We were at least on Fall Break when we scheduled our trip to Nashville. On this particular weekend, it was all about hanging out with my favorite person "My Whitney." I first noticed that soon-to-be-familiar "sinking feeling" in my stomach on Friday of the trip. I just felt like something wasn't right. I couldn't place where it was coming from. I tried to convince myself it was just odd to not be at practice when everyone else was. I don't remember a lot of details from that Friday other than eating that evening and not being able to shake the feeling something was wrong. My fears were temporarily relieved when I got a call from an assistant coach about an incident at practice. That is how uncomfortable I was—a non-injury incident at practice gave me comfort. I just knew that had to be it. That is what I told myself so I was able to at least ignore the feeling until Sunday.

***

The Titans vs. Ravens game that day was wet and cold. We showed up at the game in our "house divided" uniforms. Like I said, we both love the sport, and we follow several different NFL teams. So, I decided to support the home team, and wore my Derrick Henry Tennessee Titans jersey and my beloved Alabama ball cap since Derrick was a Heisman winner at Bama. Travis wore his Ray Lewis Ravens jersey. Sadly, the division wasn't appreciated by those around us in the stands. Rain gear and the weather thwarted our attempt to be a cute but "divided" couple. In a dreary rain, the game played on, but my mind and heart continued to race with emotions of fear, worry, and the unknown. My football loving heart was distracted. I remember the Ravens won, and Clay Walker performed "What's It To You" at half time, a real treat for us as 90s country fans. We danced and sang in our seats along with Clay, "Love is a rhythm of two hearts beating, pounding out a message steady and true. Talk to me baby, tell me what you're feeling. I know what love is, what's it to you?"[1]

As we were singing along, I noticed Travis had scratched his face and that it was bleeding. It was a tiny little scratch, but it was bleeding a good bit, even after wiping it with a cloth and applying gentle pressure. I thought that was weird, and I immediately remembered the bruises and the worry consumed me.

Again, this had happened twice in previous weeks. He had gone under the bleachers in the gym at school to retrieve a ball and gashed his back on a metal bracket on the bleachers. Fortunately, his long-time defensive coordinator, Dr. Sain was at the school and was able to get Travis cleaned up and bandaged without much of an ordeal. When Travis got home that evening and I had a chance to examine the cut, I was surprised that it also continued to bleed as soon as the bandage was removed. Then a few days later he cut his neck while shaving and the spot bled all throughout football practice that morning.

Back in the stadium on that cold, rainy October night, that gnawing feeling in my gut returned as my mind began to connect a few of the dots. Bruises, bleeding, decreased appetite, fatigue and cold intolerance. It was at this moment, the first time I thought maybe this feeling inside me isn't about the kids or life at home at all. *Is this something wrong with Travis? Is something wrong with the man I love?* The second half of the Titans vs. Ravens game is a total blur. I remember nothing that was going on except that there was an adorable little baby sitting a few rows in front of me with his mom and dad. I just watched that happy little baby boy bounce on his momma's knee and giggle. He was bundled up in Ravens gear and his eyes would light up with every swell of energy in the crowd. His innocence and pure joy were the only things that distracted me from the fear that welled up inside me. Before we left the game Travis needed to stop by the restroom before we made our trip home.

ENDNOTES

[1] Lyrics.com, STANDS4 LLC, 2022. "What's It to You Lyrics." Accessed February 24, 2022. https://www.lyrics.com/lyric/2051005/Clay+Walker.

CHAPTER 7

Blood in the Water

I stood in the corridor of the stadium near Gate A while I waited on Travis to finish up in the restroom. There was activity all around me. People busily moving around, some were going to the concession stand for warm, doughy pretzels and others were making quick trips to the restroom during television timeouts. People swirled around me while I stood there lost in thought about what was happening to my husband. It's so odd how you can be surrounded by people and feel so alone. I had my eyes locked on the men's room exit door, waiting for Travis to come out. As he exited, I caught the look on his face, and at that moment I knew there was something wrong.

When he made his way through the sea of people to where I was standing, I just said, "What's wrong?" As we began walking toward the exit gate, he said there was blood in his urine. I asked how much, and he just showed me a picture on his phone. He had actually taken a picture of the urinal because it was enough blood to turn the bowl a pale red, like watered down cranberry juice.

I've been to Nissan stadium many times in my life, including many trips to see the Titans play. Travis and I saw them play the Browns in 2016 when one of my favorite RCA Knights gave us tickets for my 30th birthday. We also saw them play the Jaguars in 2016 on Thursday Night Football because I won an online contest and was chosen to bring a plus one to be a part of the Titans Thursday Night Football Fanzone. It was one of the swankiest things I've ever witnessed. We partied with other VIP guests, ate a catered buffet, rubbed elbows with the NFL Network's Thursday Night Football cast, and brought home an awesome swag bag. We also met Ladanian Tomlinson, one of the greatest NFL running backs of all time with five Pro Bowl appearances and the 2006 NFL Most Valuable Player of the Year. And we met Eddie George, one of the best Titans players of all time, and a former Heisman Trophy winner at Ohio State University. We also got our faces on NFL Network's Thursday Night Football pregame show.

Back in 2013, we saw the Titans play the Colts with the free tickets we earned from running in the Titans Back to Football 5K that year. It was the first 5K I ever talked Travis into running with me. He only agreed to participate because he got to run through the stadium tunnel and finish the race on the 50-yard line. Oh, and there was the potential to get autographs, which is always a plus for him.

Earlier that same year in 2018, we went to Nissan Stadium and stood on the front row by the stage at the Country Music Association Music Festival thanks to Travis' friend Jeremy and his perks from working security. We jammed to Chris Stapleton, one of our favorite country music singer/songwriters. We danced and sang along to the music with a bunch of people who were a lot younger than us and stayed out way past our bedtime.

My first trip to the stadium was when I was in seventh grade. I went to see NSYNC in concert. A friend invited a big group of girls for her birthday; her parents drove us to Nashville in a rented 15-passenger van. We ate at Hard Rock Cafe on Music Row, and we listened to Pink belt some of my favorite angry girl music. We freaked out when Justin Timberlake, with his frosted curly blonde hair, floated into the crowd on a portion of the stage that moved when he sang "This I Promise You."

But, of all these memories at Nissan Stadium, the one that will live most vividly in my mind will be the look on Travis' face when he came out of that bathroom near Gate A on October 14, 2018. The look on his face told me there was something wrong, and that he was worried, but didn't want me to worry. When he told me about the blood in his urine as we were leaving the stadium and walking to our car, I told him to call Rick McCauley (one of our beloved shepherds at our church who also happens to be our doctor). Rick was out of town on vacation, but he set up an appointment for Travis to go to the clinic the next day to see one of his colleagues, Dr. Patel.

***

The next day I went to see Dr. Patel during one of my breaks at school. Dr. Patel is a short Indian man who wears his wisdom on his face. Graying hair and a facial expression that beamed kindness and care. He seemed pleased with all that he saw until he and the nurse returned to tell me that my blood count wasn't normal. As the Bible says his "countenance had fallen." I would need to see a specialist in Nashville or Huntsville. We didn't realize how fateful of a decision it would be to end up in Huntsville. After being doted on by his nurse I was out the door and headed back to school. As I began the drive back to the school from the clinic on highway 431, I began to formulate a strategy of what I was going to say to my wife, my students and football players who had a game on Friday night.

As men often do, I went with the familiar tried and true method of the downplay. I've never been one to shy away from asking for prayers, but I didn't want to worry anyone. I went to class and football practice as normal. I mentioned that I was going in for some tests and I would be poked and prodded. I admitted that I thought the doctor would need to "go deep." In all honesty, I was concerned with that inevitable biopsy that was coming. After entering the hospital my students would write me encouragement in the form of letters, cards and a giant banner that would adorn my wall. One letter stands out to me: a student of mine quoted me from Bible class. I believe we were talking about the Apostle Paul's letter to the Philippians. We were discussing enduring hardship and I said something along the lines of "Commitment to Christ is easier when you're having success but what are you going to do when you're lying in a hospital bed. The medicine they are giving you could either heal you or kill you. How committed will you be?"

If I am to be completely honest, I knew something was off for a couple of months although I can't pinpoint the exact start of those feelings. Between being a foster parent, football coach, working in church ministry, and teaching school I was tired. I thought that after 37 years my metabolism was finally slowing *down but I didn't think it could explain how I was with everyone at home. I would come home after work and was just miserable to be around. Whitney had mentioned a few times that I just didn't seem to be myself. I could not explain it. I was hoping that a weekend in Nashville over Fall Break would help me get back to my old self.*

From the moment we got there I just had a nagging feeling that something wasn't right. I now attribute that feeling to the Holy Spirit. You know I've never really had a problem with asking for directions when I got lost driving. So, I've never felt slighted by that old trope. I do however fall into the "stubborn about going to a doctor" category and I've been known to ignore the warning signs about danger in the face of having a good time. I like to stay busy, so I don't have to think about life's struggles. Believing certain situations will work themselves out can be a good thing but it almost cost me my life that time. Jesus said, "Those who are well have no need of a physician, but those who are sick. I came not to call the righteous, but sinners" (Mark 2:17, ESV). Jesus makes a reference to spiritually sick people who refused to acknowledge their need for a physician. By the Sunday before my diagnosis on Tuesday, I knew I needed a physician. Upon arriving home on Sunday night, I could tell it was dire although cancer wasn't quite where my mind went. I thank God for ignorance sometimes, although I was not in any hurry to put two and two together.

It was a weird sort of relief to know I was going to get some answers as to why I felt the way I felt. Although I'd have to wait until the next day. I went home and tried my best to not let Whitney see how distraught I was. I've never been very good and hiding my feelings. It was a rollercoaster because in front of her, I'd do my best to swallow the gut-wrenching nausea of the unknown. I remember watching Monday Night Football in hopes that my favorite sport might dull the pain. Aaron Rodgers and his familiar yellow with green and white logo gave me no relief. It's crazy how something you enjoy so much becomes so meaningless. Meaningless in a one-man pity party.

CHAPTER 8

Wrestling with God

I didn't go with Travis to his appointment with Dr. Patel; looking back I can't believe I wasn't there with him. I guess I still didn't believe that anything could seriously be wrong because he seemed to be in such good health. I just remember sitting in my office and getting a phone call from Travis that afternoon. There were only three of us left in the office, myself, my co-worker, Krysa, and the principal, Cara. I don't remember what we were working on, but the three of us were huddled in my office around my computer when I got the call. He said Dr. Patel and his nurse was setting him up for an appointment with a "specialist" the next day because his white blood cell count was high, and they needed to know if we wanted to go to Huntsville or Nashville. I said Huntsville quickly, still not thinking anything was seriously wrong with him. I just knew he had a JV football game to coach the next day and we would never make it back in time from Nashville for the game.

I went home that afternoon and had a meeting with our kids' new developmental therapist. The kids had been in developmental therapy for about a year at that point. I have explained to you that Hailee and Daniel came to us through the foster care system, but I haven't fully explained all the difficulties that come along with caring for children who have been through trauma. We learned in our foster care certification classes about the effects that trauma can have on a child's development. We even learned that every time a child is moved from home to home, they are set back six months developmentally. As we began caring for the kids in 2017, we started to see more and more signs of developmental delays. Fortunately, the state of Tennessee has an early intervention program for children under the age of 4. The state will evaluate children for developmental delays and provide in-home therapies free of charge for children who need help.

Our friend Tori was their first developmental therapist, and she had been instrumental in helping smooth out *so* many of our daily household routines and taught us different tricks for communicating that had made life so much easier. So, this meeting was very important, but my mind was not there at all. I could only think about what a "specialist" might mean. I assumed a hematologist because of Travis' bleeding and the bruises, but I didn't know at the time that hematologists are also oncologists.

When Travis got home from football that day, he was obviously worried. I have explained that Travis loves fun, he reframes anything that is bad and puts it in a positive light and is always the life of the party. The man that came through the door that evening around dinner time was not the fun, carefree man that keeps me from taking myself and the world too seriously. I had never seen Travis that way before; he was obviously worried and very tearful. In fact, after we put the kids to bed, we sat down, and he just held me and cried. He never actually let me know all the details of his visit with Dr. Patel until days later, but he had a good idea that whatever was wrong could kill him. I couldn't even bring myself to ask.

That night I didn't sleep a wink. I would doze for a minute or two then I would jerk awake with an intense fear that I could lose everyone in my little family before the end of the year if Travis was very sick and the kiddos went home to their mom. That's a sobering thought, and it was very real. I tossed and turned in the bed that night, oscillating between being mad at God for doing this to my family and begging Him to take care of them.

The next day Travis and I went to work even though our boss, the Head of School at RCA, had told us we could take off the whole day. We both knew the day would be easier if we weren't just sitting still and had responsibilities to keep us busy. We left school around lunch and came home to eat before heading to Huntsville for the 1:00 PM appointment. Neither one of us really ate anything. We heated up some leftovers, but I think we both just kind of pushed it around on the plate.

The drive was miserable. A constant rain pounded the whole time. My mind was still swirling with "what ifs." *What if Travis is really sick? What if he dies? What if he suffers? What if the kids go home? What if the kids are not ok? What if I'm left all alone? What if I fall into a deep depression and never recover?* I tried to remind myself it was senseless to put myself through this turmoil when we didn't even know what his diagnosis was; I was only making myself live through the trauma in my head, when none of it had actually happened yet.

When we arrived at the doctor's office, we didn't know that the building had a free valet service due to the lack of parking, so we parked in a spot that was about as far from the entrance door as you could get. Travis grabbed my hand and said a prayer. I can't remember exactly what he prayed, but I do remember that he prayed that we would walk faithfully, no matter the news. I didn't like the sound of that. It sounded like he was expecting news I didn't want to hear. We got out of the car and splashed through the cold puddles while huddled under one tiny pink umbrella. When we made it across the parking lot to the entrance, we went straight to the elevator and up to the fourth floor. When those elevator doors opened, my heart dropped from my chest to my stomach. On the wall in front of my eyes was the word I feared most: *Cancer.*

The wall said Clearview Cancer Institute (CCI), and the cancer word was right in front of my face. Even when I saw those words, I didn't *truly* believe that it could happen to us, but it was. At that time, we still had no idea that Travis had seen our home for what would be the last time until Thanksgiving.

CHAPTER 9

The "C" Word

October 16, 2018 was the day I heard my husband had leukemia. It was a rainy, and an uncharacteristically cold Tuesday for October in the South. When Travis checked in at the front desk at CCI, the secretary handed him a new patient packet and a lot of paperwork to fill out and then sent him to the back for labs. I thought, *he just did blood work yesterday, why would they possibly need more blood, and we're not going to be needing all this cancer information in this booklet about managing chemotherapy side effects.*

After Travis came back from the lab, he started on the mound of paperwork. I noticed his leg bounced the whole time he worked on it; he can never stop moving anyway, but his leg has a different bounce to it when he is nervous. I knew this was the nervous bounce, not the "I'm-full-of-energy-and-always-looking-for-the-next-fun-thing-bounce." When he was done with the paperwork, the secretary had us visit the financial aid department. My first thought at this point was, *we don't have time for all this. He's got to coach a JV football game in a couple of hours. We need to see this doctor and get his medicine and go. They should save this information for those people out there in the lobby who are obviously really sick.* I had no idea my husband was sicker at that moment than probably anyone else in the lobby.

***

My first visit with my oncologist involved a lot of paperwork, poking, prodding and getting my picture taken (yes, I was smiling in the picture). While all of this was going on I noticed an older gentleman make his way out of the treatment area and ring a bell attached to the left of the exit. Prior to his ringing of the bell, all the nurses and volunteers piled out into the hallway. They got their phones out to document the event as the gentlemen celebrated the end of his treatments with the traditional ringing of the bell. I remember thinking how many times they'd have to replace that bell if the patients had been strong enough to ring it off the wall in joyous celebration. Then the thought of how satisfying that feeling must have been ran across my mind. At that point I had no real understanding of just how much that older gentleman and I would have in common.

***

A nice gentleman named Matt came to get us from the lobby. He was a younger looking man, maybe in his 40s, wearing scrubs and glasses. I immediately noticed he had a big tattoo of an orange ribbon on his forearm and that he had a kind smile that put me at ease. He took Travis to a small room where they took his blood pressure and weighed him. He weighed 153 pounds; it hit me that he had lost at least ten pounds since the summer because I remembered him bragging about his "size" and wishing he had been that "big" when he played high school football. That worried me a little. He had lost the weight slowly, so I didn't notice it so much, but ten pounds on a person his size is significant in that amount of time.

When Matt took us down the hallway to Dr. Diaz's examination room, I noticed a bookshelf with mannequin heads all adorned with wigs or hats and a sign that said "Free, take one." Those few hours seem like an out-of-body experience. I can remember seeing all these things and hearing words come from the doctors and nurses, but not fully processing or understanding what all this meant for our life. I was becoming increasingly aware that all these people were fighting cancer either in their own bodies or supporting loved ones in their fight, and from the looks of things they thought we were joining their club. I still didn't want to believe this was happening to Travis, to us.

When we were seated in the exam room, I looked at all the literature on the walls. Literature about every kind of cancer and treatment options, chemotherapy support groups, classes concerning how to deal with medication side effects, etc. It was overwhelming. I can remember my heart felt like it was racing in my chest like I had just finished sprinting the last quarter of a mile of a 5K and my whole body felt tingly.

After a few minutes Dr. Diaz came in. I first noticed the expression on his face, and I didn't like it. He was a young man with brown skin, thick, shiny black hair, and he wore a white coat with his name embroidered on the front left chest. His deep brown eyes told me he was worried and had news he didn't want to deliver. He held papers in his hands. I assumed it was the result of the lab work Travis had when we got there. I assumed correctly. He told Travis to sit on the exam table and asked him a few questions about his symptoms like when they had started, and the medications he had taken. Then he had Travis take off his shirt so he could get a look at all the bruising. He had him put his shirt back on and told him he could get down. Travis sat next to me again, and he delivered the news I had dreaded hearing.

> Based on your bloodwork and what I can see from your symptoms, you have leukemia. Your white count doubled since you had bloodwork done yesterday. I don't know what kind of leukemia it is yet, but I'm going to take a look at your blood cells under a microscope. That will give me an idea, but we have to do a bone marrow biopsy to know for sure. We're going to move you across the hallway in a second to get that done," with those words, he paused and took a breath, and then looked at me before continuing. "If this is the type of leukemia I suspect, you need to know that we will be admitting Travis to the hospital probably tomorrow, and you need to plan for him staying for weeks, not days.

With that said, he opened the door and left quietly with

his head down for us to process this news alone. I completely broke down. The kind of crying where you can't catch your breath. Travis was resolute. He didn't cry. He wasn't angry. He was a rock. I felt terrible because I should have been the one being strong for him, but he was holding it together for me. We didn't have much time to process anything, or let anyone know, or talk about the next step, or how we were feeling because Dr. Diaz's nurse, Mrs. Pat, came in shortly. She too looked very sorry for what we were going through. She offered me a box of tissues and began paperwork for the bone marrow biopsy. She moved us across the hallway to a room that was set up for the procedure.

***

I texted the toughest woman I've ever known, my mom. Doris Creasy raised three boys with a lot of help from my aunts, uncles, church family and coaches. The toughest woman I know begat the toughest man I've ever known, my older brother Bradley. Bradley was born 6 years before me. He was diagnosed with Cerebral Palsy at a young age and has battled brittle bones and life-threatening circumstances all his life. I've watched him go from a healthy-looking child who had the meanest chokehold I've experienced outside of Lonnie Jones to his body being bent and broken, but he continues to thrive. He has scars from a broken hip, femur, a head injury, a metal rod that keeps his lungs from collapsing and has a feeding tube. He takes medication for seizures and can smile through it all. When he gained a little bit of freedom with a motorized wheelchair it didn't take him long to use it as a weapon and he tried to run me over, in true older brother fashion. Bradley is my half-brother, but we are so close it's difficult to remember that distinction. He's inspired me through any turmoil in my life; cancer would be no different. Bradley is one of many touchstones that God has provided. Because of his Cerebral Palsy, Bradley has never spoken a word but like me he does not have much of a poker face. He might be the most honest person that has never uttered a word. It's all on his face. As tough as Bradley is, his emotional support is our mom.

In the text, I asked my mom if she was still on her mail route. She was a rural route carrier for the Florence, Alabama area. She was a mail carrier for as long as I can remember before retiring shortly after my diagnosis. My mother is a hard worker. She was always grateful for her job at the post office and worked every day so she could put food on the table. At one point while my dad was laid off, she took another job at Burger King. We didn't understand how tired she was but we sure were fired up when she brought leftover fries home!

I've been blessed with strong women in my life. I had the wonderful Whitney beside me and to be honest, I wanted my momma there too. I needed all the support I could get especially from people who had made tough decisions in the past. Mom had faced many challenges and made many tough choices. From surgery decisions to allowing Bradley to move into El Reposo Nursing Home when he was a teen. Looking back, they all seem like the right decisions, although she might not consider them decisions so much as necessities. I too wouldn't have a decision to make as my treatment would be a dire necessity.

Before she replied, I texted my childhood best friend and cousin Ben that I had leukemia. As I read his reply, "You're joking," my mom responded that she was not on her route, and

I called her. I can't remember the exact words, but she didn't want to believe me. It's understandable because I didn't want to believe me. Oddly enough the event that I was the most anxious about was the bone marrow biopsy which was soon to be a reality.

CHAPTER 10

Going Deep

They laid Travis on his side on the table and began preparing him for a biopsy. I began texting a few people; my parents, our boss, and a couple of friends including Debbie and Phil who were taking care of our kids. Travis handed me his phone and had me contact his coaches to tell them they would have to go on without him. It's funny. I had completely forgotten about the JV football game I was so worried about getting home in time for. I just remember typing the message to several people, "Please pray. It's bad. He has leukemia. They're doing a bone marrow biopsy now. He will be in the hospital for several weeks."

I also told my mom not to tell my sister Bailey because she was in labor, bringing my sweet nephew, John Luke, into the world. She had an appointment with her OBGYN at the exact same time as Travis' appointment with Dr. Diaz. Before we knew anything about his diagnosis, Bailey texted me to say that they were admitting her to induce labor because her blood pressure was so high. She was induced at the exact same time Dr. Diaz began Travis' biopsy.

Mr. Bryant, our boss, asked if he could alert the faculty and staff via email. I asked him to wait because my sister didn't know yet. I did not want my coworkers to know before our family knew, and I didn't want the news to start spreading via social media before my sister found out. I remember thinking later that I could never have experienced as much sorrow and joy, mourning and dancing in the same moments. I was so happy for my sister and my brother-in-law Dalton.

Bailey had suffered a miscarriage the year before and it was a devastating loss. She had been through so much and grieved the loss of her first baby. She was so excited when she found out she was pregnant with John Luke, but she still worried because of her first loss. She and Dalton didn't even find out John Luke's gender until the birth. They were both just so happy to have a healthy baby after their first loss that they decided to wait and be surprised at the birth.

I had been looking forward to being there for the birth and experiencing the excitement with my family when we found out the baby's gender. I knew it would be a moment I would never forget. I *never* expected the day Bailey gave birth would live so clearly in my memory for a different reason.

When we think back on that day, Bailey always says that she learned no one in our family has a good poker face. She says every time she asked if Travis and I would be there, everyone just kind of looked around with sad and bewildered expressions on their faces. I was so elated that her day had finally come. She would finally hold her baby in her arms. God was bringing beauty from ashes. But I also mourned in my heart. I mourned the pain Travis was enduring as Dr. Diaz drove a thick, hollow needle in his hip. I mourned the fact that life would never be the same, I mourned because I was missing the arrival of Bailey's baby.

***

Today I'm encouraged every time I see John Luke. He is a constant reminder that life goes on and thrives even among the darkest of times. For a long time, I felt a lot of shame that I had rained on the little guy's parade. It was supposed to be their day. We were supposed to meet him as soon as possible. It would be delayed but I was bound and determined to get out of the hospital. I'd meet him for the first time 4-5 weeks later, on Thanksgiving Day. While Whitney was doing her best to keep the worst kept secret from reaching her sister's notice, I was in the middle of doing my impersonation of a pin cushion.

It seems like the Holy Spirit was preparing me for a bone marrow biopsy for days if not weeks. I just knew. The best description on how it feels is if you've ever taken a flat head screwdriver and used it to wedge open a paint can, except that paint can is your hip. It felt like that tube was the large flat head and it seemed like my hip was going to pop out of socket.

***

Travis laid on that table and quoted Romans 8:18 to himself, "For I consider that the sufferings of this present time are not worth comparing with the glory that is to be revealed to us." Romans 8 is his favorite chapter from the whole Bible, so it's not surprising this was the scripture that provided him the most comfort at a time of such intense pain.

They didn't have the capability to sedate him at the doctor's office for the procedure, so they just used local anesthesia. I could tell it was painful even with the anesthesia. When the biopsy was completed, Dr. Diaz asked Matt to apply pressure to help the bleeding stop.

I thank God I didn't understand that there should not have been so much blood. I guess ignorance is bliss in that situation because I just assumed there should be lots of blood after a procedure like that. I didn't realize Travis' ability to clot was next to nothing.

Matt applied pressure for several minutes. I don't remember how long, but the office was closing by this time. We were the last patients left. After a while, Dr. Diaz came in, looked at the puncture area and the blood, and said he was having Pat get admittance papers for the hospital ready at that moment. So, the game plan changed. We would not return home for the night; we would be going straight to the hospital without a night in our own home to process the situation. We didn't even have a bag with any belongings for the long stay.

Mrs. Pat eventually came into the room with an envelope and handed it to me. It was thick with paperwork for Travis' admittance. She gave me instructions to drive under the main awning of Huntsville Hospital on Gallatin Street. She assured me that a valet would park our car and told me to go straight through the revolving doors to the admittance desk and hand the person at the desk the envelope she had given me. Matt and Mrs. Pat wrapped a sheet around Travis to keep the blood from getting all over our car.

As we made our way out of the fourth-floor office, I noticed everything looked very different from when we had arrived earlier. I'm not sure what time it was or how long we had been there, but we were the only people left in the office. All the staff members, nurses, and doctors had left for the day. The lights were turned off. The televisions in the lobby were off. There was silence everywhere. It was a stark contrast to what was going on in my mind and body.

My mind bounced from thought to thought. Should we have gotten an ambulance? Is Travis ok to walk? How am I going to do this? How am I going to take care of the kids, work, *and* be there for Travis? What is the fastest way to get to the hospital? Then the thoughts from the night before would rear their ugly heads. *What if I lose them all? What if Travis doesn't make it? What if he suffers? What if the kids go home? What if I'm left all alone? What if I fall into a deep depression that I never recover from?*

My body trembled. Maybe it was really more like a shiver. I remember seeing my hand shake as I reached out to take the envelope from Mrs. Pat. I did my best to still it, but that shivering, trembling, shaking feeling was making its rounds through my body. When I felt like I had it under control, it would come over me like a cold chill and send ripples of anxious tremors throughout my body.

We went down the elevator, and I told Travis to wait on me in the lobby while I pulled the car around to pick him up. I was worried that he would pass out from the blood loss if he traipsed across the parking lot through the cold puddles and the dark and dreary rain that continued to steadily pound. I popped the small pink umbrella up and stepped out into the rain and ran through the cold puddles to where we had parked the car hours earlier. When I reached the back of the parking lot, I located our black Nissan Armada and hopped in the driver seat. I quickly pushed the seat heater buttons. I thought the least I could do was make sure Travis had a warm seat on our drive to the hospital where we would spend the next 37 days; I also hoped it would knock the chill off my body I had not been able to shake. That was futile. The chilling tremors of anxiety continued to plague me through that night and the next day. As I drove the car across the parking lot to pick Travis up, I remember thinking that life had drastically changed in the few hours since I sat in that car the last time. I also remembered thinking about the prayer Travis had offered before we went in. The one part of his prayer I did not like was the one thing that brought comfort, and I continually offered it as a prayer to God over the next weeks, "Lord, whatever happens, help us to walk faithfully."

CHAPTER 11

Red Sea Moment

When I drove underneath the awning to pick Travis up, the security guard told me he was bleeding a lot. He looked very concerned, and even questioned if I should be driving him. I assured him that his doctor had given us orders to take him to Huntsville Hospital where he would be admitted. He reluctantly said ok and helped Travis into the car and packed the sheet around him that was soaking up the blood.

The drive from Dr. Diaz's office to Huntsville Hospital is a short one no matter what route you take. I decided to take Whitesburg Drive. Every time I drive that road nowadays, the conversation we had on the way to the hospital comes back to my mind, and I'm in awe at what God can do when our circumstances look very bleak.

You see, I felt like we were at a Red Sea moment. I couldn't see any way out just like the Israelites when they approached the Red Sea after God set them free from 400 years of slavery in Egypt. God worked ten miracles in the form of science-defying signs that proved his sovereignty, power, and commitment to His people. He led them out of Egypt, and brought them to the Red Sea, but it was there where their faith was tested first. The Israelites saw there was no way through the sea, and the Egyptian army with all their soldiers and chariots were closing in on them from behind. All they saw were their bleak circumstances, and what looked like death either by drowning or the Egyptian sword. *But God*. God defied scientific odds again and sent a mighty wind to blow back the sea until it stood like two walls on each side of his Covenant People as they walked through the middle on dry ground. God can make a way where our human eyes see no way, and my human eyes saw no way that we could continue to care for our two foster babies amid this cancer diagnosis and treatment.

Hailee and Daniel had been in our home for 18 months to the day. They had arrived at our home on Easter Sunday, April 16, 2017. This was October 16, 2018. I thought about their little faces, and what they may be doing at that exact moment at Paw Paw and Bebbie's (Phillip and Debbie, our friends from church) house. Maybe they were eating their favorite foods like pancakes or spaghetti. Maybe they were watching Mickey Mouse Clubhouse or Paw Patrol on Debbie's TV in the upstairs loft. Maybe they were racing each other up and down the stairs. Maybe they were helping Paw Paw feed the cows. Maybe they were chasing Bear or Barbosa, the cats. Since day one, Paw Paw and Bebbie had been a part of their "village." Debbie was one of the ladies who had volunteered to babysit while I was at work before they could get a spot in a daycare. They had graciously volunteered to keep the kids while we went to Travis' doctor appointment that afternoon. I didn't have any suspicions we wouldn't make it home in time to pick them up from daycare, but Dr. McCauley did. He advised us to find someone to take care of the kids in case we were running late after the appointment.

My mind drifted to how far we had come in the 18 months since their arrival. We had gone from complete strangers to a family. We were spending our days wrangling our sassy and tenacious three-year-old daughter and our wild but loving two-year-old son. Hailee was a lot like Travis. She loved a good party or celebration. In fact, anytime there was a change of seasonal decor at our house she got very excited, and asked, "is it almost time to celebrate?!?" She was an early riser; waking up every day excited about life and wondering what fun things she was going to participate in. She was a good consistency monitor as well; she would put her hand on her hip in a hot second and remind you, "You said...." with her pretty blue eyes staring intently.

Daniel was full of energy and was all boy. He was always imagining that his toys were swords, and he loved the "bad guys" in every movie, especially Captain Hook. He loved Daddy's "Football Boys" and was pretty sure that he could take any of them down on his own, even though he only weighed in at a whopping 25 pounds. He had a naturally perfect-form tackle, and unfortunately practiced it frequently on his sister. We figured out that when he began to grit his teeth, someone was going down, so most of the time we could intercede before Sissy or the dog wound up on the wrong side of the tackle drill. His "inside voice" was everyone else's "stadium voice" and he was constantly on the go, but his heart was loving and kind. He was always quick to remind me to read our morning devotional at breakfast and to pray for those who are hurting, and he gave the best cuddly hugs.

We had fallen in love with these babies, especially since we had been caring for them so long. We were devastated at the thought that our future may not include them, but that was the way things were looking. I was already in a state of near constant anxiety over the thought that they could possibly return to their first home soon. My heart ached at the thought of the silence my home would echo without their playful shrieks of delight and heavy-footed running. My eyes would well with tears when I thought of them reaching milestones like riding a bike, losing a tooth, learning to read, and putting their faith and trust in Jesus even though I may never know or see any of it.

At the moment, all I knew was that Travis was my forever family, my beloved husband, and I wanted to be fully present for him during this trial. It would be tough being there for him and taking care of the kids with all the demands and limitations imposed by the foster system. We couldn't ask just *anyone* to babysit the children, they couldn't travel across state lines or miss too much daycare. They had to be in town for visits with biological parents, and be available to meet with CASA workers, DCS case managers, and continue with their developmental and speech therapy. It was a daunting task to figure out with all our family living out-of-state.

I didn't want to add another worry to Travis' load, but I knew we had to talk about it. So, I reluctantly brought it up on the drive down Whitesburg Drive toward Huntsville Hospital. I remember saying with a lot of hesitancy, "I know you don't want to hear this right now, but I'm just not sure we can keep the kids. I feel like I may need to call the case manager and tell her she may need to look for another placement option for them."

To my relief, Travis said he had been thinking the same thing; I was glad it was already on his radar, but I had been secretly hoping he saw a solution I hadn't come up with yet. My heart felt like it was being wrenched open. I remember the trauma they had to overcome when they were removed from their biological parents' home and placed in ours. Their whole world was turned upside down. Now, they were thriving little toddlers who loved life and everyone they met. Their village was full of loving extended family members including aunts, uncles, grandparents, great-grandparents, cousins, and friends who were more like family, and it was all about to be ripped out from under them...again.

It just wasn't fair. All the praying I had been doing for the last several months, holding them both in my lap while they wiggled and squirmed every night and asking God to do immeasurable good for their futures seemed to have been in a vain; they were simply words tossed against the fluffy pink floral pillows that adorned Hailee's bed. This certainly didn't seem like the immeasurable good I had in mind for them.

CHAPTER 12

Be Still

I slid out of our black Armada and I waddled into the Huntsville Hospital main entrance. There I was with several white blankets wrapped around me from the waist down. I could feel the blood drip from my hip, down my leg and pool in the heel of my shoe. Interestingly enough, it did not seem like an odd scene for the hurried pace of the hospital. One person offered me help but I turned them down. As I sit here writing this, I know I should've been shouting for help. I don't know if I was out of oxygen, energy or just low on blood; maybe all the above. I continued my zombie trek to the admitting area. I sat down in the green chairs which I'm sure are typically cozy and inviting. However, when you have a hole in your hip, they aren't so comfy. I got the attention of someone, showed them my mess, and admonished if they didn't want a mess on their floor, I needed to see someone quickly. She moved me to an office where someone was being trained in admitting. The sweet lady was training a young man who as I recall was working the "hunt and peck" method of typing my info into the computer. I once again tried to communicate that unless *they wanted to pick me up out of the floor, covered in my own blood, I needed to get moved. They hurriedly brought a wheelchair in and rushed me up to the 7th floor.*

One of the most awkward moments of my life was being cleaned up in the bathroom. The female nurse who had the unlucky task of cleaning up all the blood was an acquaintance of mine. She had dated one of my football players. Add in the fact that my wife was standing right outside the door made this incredibly awkward. To make matters worse, I opened my mouth. I mentioned that she was familiar to me and made the connection that she was the fiancé of my former player. I don't think she thought it important at the moment to tell me, but I later realized she had been but was not currently his fiancé. Oddly enough, emergency situations cut through all that awkward small talk.

Before too long, the room was swamped with nurses scrambling to get blood and platelets into my veins. I became a human pin cushion as I began to think every nurse in the building was going to take a run at me. My veins were nearly invisible. They finally brought an ultrasound machine to find one. At some point a nurse brought in a tightly wound ball of sheets and tucked it under my hip to keep the pressure on my biopsy puncture. I attempted to sleep on that thing all night long. I've never longed for a night of wrestling with God like the Old Testament patriarch Jacob (Genesis 32:22-32). I have been known to enjoy the occasional pro wrestling match. I've been to two WrestleMania's, but nothing prepared me for wrestling with that superball of uncomfortableness. It felt like a boulder but it was probably the size of a basketball or soccer ball. It was my first run in with the dreaded "Mr. Creasy you need to rest but we will be back in thirty minutes to wake you

up to see how you are resting" approach. Now I understand
they were trying to keep me alive and I appreciate it greatly.
At the time my discomfort was all I could think about, and it
took the shape of the perceived "Rock of Gibraltar" stabbing my
hip. The battle had only begun.

***

Very soon after the nurses got Travis cleaned and in bed,
there were a handful of family and friends already making
their way to the hospital. Our friend Michael Rosenblum
was there almost immediately. It was such a comfort to see
another familiar face. Michael must have left work and come
straight to the hospital; his real estate office was only a few
miles away.

Debbie and Phil called to tell me the kids could stay with
them as long as we needed them to. I gave them instructions
on where to find an extra key at our house, where the kids'
clothes were located, and all the miscellaneous things scattered throughout the house that would make the kids' stay
with them more comfortable. I was so thankful to have "the
village" of people around us who loved our children like
their own, and with whom the kids felt comfortable. It put
my mind at ease to know they were safe and taken care of in
a home with people they loved dearly.

Dr. Diaz made it to the hospital very quickly too. I
didn't know if it was normal practice for the oncologist to
follow his patient to the hospital, but it seemed atypical.
Dr. Diaz seemed very invested in Travis' wellbeing and it
gave me a lot of comfort. He talked to us about the "plan"
for the night and the next day, which included another

bone marrow biopsy under guided radiology because he had not been able to get what he needed in the office due to Travis' excessive bleeding, many scans of Travis' organs to make sure that there was no internal bleeding, lots of blood transfusions and platelets, and a dose of All Trans Retinoic Acid (ATRA) that would help fix his white blood cells.

When he was finished speaking, he asked if we had any questions, the only thing I could think to mention was that I was worried about Travis' foot (of all the things), I had noticed when he took his bloody shoe off that his foot was blue and swollen. It had not been like that earlier in the day. Dr. Diaz pulled Travis' blanket back, and picked up his foot carefully, examined it, and rubbed his hand over it. He laid Travis' foot down on the bed again, and carefully covered it with the blanket. When he looked up, there was a new sense of urgency about him.

He seemed more intense and definitely more hurried. He said this lined up with the diagnosis that he had suspected, and that it would be important for him to start the ATRA as soon as possible because it is the main treatment for that particular leukemia. I later learned the reason for Dr. Diaz's urgency was that a diagnosis of Acute Promyelocytic Leukemia is considered a medical emergency because of the high risk the patient could bleed out.

I heard him give the nurses instructions concerning Travis' care and remember him bringing a packet of information about the ATRA medication he was going to start. I also remember hearing him tell the nurses to call him if anything changed with Travis. I felt very secure in the oncologist we landed, and I was thankful to God because I could tell there was no time to question if we were doing the right thing or if we had the right doctor.

Travis' brother Kevin and his wife Melissa happened to be in Huntsville at the time, and they made it to the hospital very quickly. My uncle was at the door soon after them. I have no idea how they even found out what room Travis was in. I'm pretty sure I didn't even know the room number. I had been too preoccupied with actually getting him situated to care.

I know Kevin and Melissa's presence was a comfort to Travis. I remember him asking Kevin to call their dad and tell him what was going on. I felt a sense of relief to have at least one blood relative there. My uncle Lee was one of the few family members I had who lived nearby that wasn't at the hospital in Boaz awaiting the birth of little John Luke.

My friends Britney and Josh were there very quickly, and they stayed a long time with us. I believe they were there until the hospital administration began making announcements to run visitors out for the evening. As the minutes went on, more and more people began to trickle in to offer us their love, support, and prayers. I've never been so thankful for friends, family, and most importantly the Lord's church. It was overwhelming in the very best of ways.

I remember seeing Jim Black and Daniel Eldridge coming down the hallway. They are long-time Riverside family. They are two of the three men responsible for us being at RCA in the first place. In 2007, they along with Chris Jones pursued Travis as a campus minister, football coach, and Bible teacher until there really wasn't another excuse to offer them. I have been thankful for their stubborn tenacity many times over the last 14 years. They visited with us, and prayed for Travis. Travis' eyes welled with tears when Jim spoke.

Mrs. Vicky Herston also came that night. I remember seeing an attractive, silver-haired woman coming down the hallway with a pink and white striped tote on her arm while I was bidding Jim and Daniel farewell for the night. She looked familiar, but I couldn't place her face; she was out of context for me. Then she spoke and called me by name. I realized that she was one of the sweet ladies from Jacksonburg Church of Christ, my mother-in-law's church. I had seen her and spent time with her many times at church homecoming services. She handed me the pink and white tote, and asked if Doris had made it yet and how Travis was doing. The tote was full of hospital necessities like snacks, a blanket, and a good novel. I was so struck that this kind woman, who I didn't know very well, would drop everything, pack a hospital bag for us, and make her way to downtown Huntsville on a cold and rainy night to bring it to us. Mrs. Vicky was one of my favorite visitors throughout the long hospital duration. I'm not sure how many times she came to visit and encourage us, but I would guess that it was about once per week. Her presence was warm and friendly, and she was especially helpful because she was a retired nurse.

My Aunt Lesa and Uncle David made their way to Huntsville to visit with us that night too. Lesa brought a pillow that I ended up sleeping on every night I was there. It's actually still on my bed at home. It was so much more comfortable than the flat scratchy pillows the hospital offered. I was happy to have Lesa and David there, because Lesa kept me informed on everything that was happening in

Boaz with Bailey while I talked to everyone who was coming and going and filled people in on what had happened, what the doctor had said, and what the plan for the next day or so was.

I was also frantically trying to answer all the text messages and phone calls I was receiving all while trying to keep too many people from finding out what was going on. I feared that Bailey would find out from the wrong person or that she would find out before she was able to deliver John Luke. In fact, at one point I remember getting a text from our boss, Mr. Bryant asking for a second time if he could go ahead and alert the staff via email because he had seen where the news had broken on Facebook by a third party.

Thankfully, it was only a few minutes later when Lesa burst out with the words, "It's a *boy*!"

I let out a huge sigh of relief, followed by a shout of joy, then the declaration, "I knew it, I knew it, I knew it!"

When it got time for the kiddos to go to bed, Debbie called to let us talk before she put them down for the night. I had filled her in earlier on what was happening, and she was quick to say they could stay with her. My heart ached again, just hearing their little voices, and thinking about the conversation I was going to have the next day with their case manager. It was very difficult not to cry ugly tears with all the people standing around me in the tiny hospital room.

After talking to the kids, I realized I had to get my dog Landry taken care of. The kiddos were safe and comfortable at Debbie and Paw Paw's house for the night, but Landry was at home with no one to feed her or let her out, and it looked like it would be that way for a while. Everyone had been asking what they could do to help, but I hadn't been able to think of anything, yet. When I realized Landry couldn't take care of herself at home, I asked my uncle Lee and my friend Britney the biggest favors I could come up with. I asked if Lee could keep Landry at his house, and if Britney would drive her there. You need to know Lee already has one large, very active white Labrador retriever and three kids. I was asking him to add another very large golden retriever to the mix. He said yes without hesitating. You also need to know that Britney is not a fan of large dogs, especially large dogs who want to be in your face, but she followed me all the way to our house across the state line in Fayetteville and brought Landry back to Lee's house in Huntsville, a 45-minute drive.

Britney and I left the hospital around 9:00 p.m. She followed me so she could get Landry and so I could get some stuff Travis and I would need for the hospital stay. I shivered the whole way home while I listened to Lauren Daigle's *Look Up Child* album. I remember thinking about how appropriate it was that Lauren had released this new album just a few weeks prior. Her first album had brought me through my most recent difficult spiritual season when we became foster parents. *How Can It Be* was the soundtrack for our early days of foster care; the days where we were so physically tired and so emotionally exhausted that it was all we could do to put one foot in front of the other. The songs on *Look Up Child* became our morning playlist every day for the next 37 days. It was a ritual that brought hope and made us feel held.

When I made it home, I gathered all the things I could think of that we would need. Britney helped me; she had more wits about her than I did at the moment. She reminded me of several things I would have forgotten without her help. After gathering everything, I said goodbye to Landry as I put her in the back of Britney and Josh's car, and then made my way back to the hospital.

On the way back to Huntsville, I gave my mom a call. I hadn't really been able to talk to her yet. I remember telling her I was worried about us financially, but I knew it would all be ok just as long as Travis was ok. I also broke the news to her that I thought we would have to give up the kids. She pushed back. She rattled off some solutions, all of which wouldn't work for various reasons—I had already tried to maneuver them in my head. I could tell she was as devastated as me at the thought of losing them. She did at least get me to agree to not call the kids' case manager until we knew what Travis' actual diagnosis was, and what the plan would be for his treatment.

The rest of that night is a restless blur of alarms beeping and nurses running. Me and Doris, Travis' mother, slept on a tiny "window seat" that pulled out to a make-shift bed. It wasn't even the width or length of a twin bed. Every time Travis seemed to get to a point of restful breathing, and I dozed a bit, the alarms on his IV unit started beeping wildly and the nurses would come running to check it out. He was going through blood, platelets, and fluids so quickly, it seemed like they were hanging new bags every 30 minutes.

I tried praying, and the only thing that came to me was, "Help us, God." I didn't have any other words. I just trusted that the Holy Spirit was interceding for me, as Paul writes in Romans 8:26-27, "The Spirit helps us in our weakness. For we do not know what to pray for as we ought, but the Spirit himself intercedes for us with groanings too deep for words.

And he who searches hearts knows what is the mind of the Spirit, because the Spirit intercedes for the saints according to the will of God." I had no words at the moment to express my fears, pain, or hopes. I was exhausted and my heart was broken.

All I knew was that we needed the hand of *Jehovah-Rapha* on our lives at that moment. I have developed an obsession for Children's Bibles since Hailee and Daniel came to live with us. There are four Children's Bibles on Hailee's bookshelf right now. A good Children's Bible has enough theological meaning for an adult to jump off the diving board in the deep end of the Bible study pool, while remaining shallow enough for a child to splash and play at the same time. I rotate which one I read to the kids each night, and one of my favorite Bibles in the stack is called *I AM: 40 Reasons to Trust God*. Each of the 40 stories reveals a different name of God and aspect of his character. *Jehovah-Rapha* means the Lord Who Heals. The story doesn't only reveal that God is a healer of physical bodies, but also the healer of our mental, emotional, and spiritual brokenness.

I remember for months leading up to October 16, 2018, I had advocated in every way I knew how for my babies. I had kept detailed records, sent emails, made phone calls, prayed, asked others to pray, and prayed some more. I obsessively kept records of everything I felt would help plead their case when the time came.

The night of Travis' diagnosis, I sat in the recliner in his first hospital room, next to his bed while the alarms rang out and nurses whizzed in and out, and I knew then and there that my obsessive record-keeping and communication with DCS officials and anyone else who would listen to me was over. I sat there in that chair, looked down at my cell phone, and told God that I couldn't do both of these things. I could not be in this hospital room and give Travis the support he needed and continue to play the part of the "squeaky wheel" on behalf of the children. I told God that I knew he loved them more than I did. I told God that I trusted the prayers I had prayed in Hailee's bedroom floor with both kids piled in my lap had not gone unnoticed. I told God he had to take over in this fight because I couldn't do it anymore.

You know what he said?

"Finally. Now stand back and watch me take care of all the things you've obsessed and fretted over for months."

In essence, I feel like God told me the same thing Moses told the Israelites at the Red Sea when they had nowhere to go. The sea was in front of them, and the Egyptian army was closing in behind them, and Moses said, "The Lord himself will fight for you, just be still" (Exodus 14:14).

That verse became a mantra for us. I guess if you've read Mark Batterson's book, *The Circle Maker*, you could say that we "circled that promise" from scripture. When the students from Riverside sent cards to the hospital room, we hung them all over the walls. Exodus 14:14 was written on one of them in bright calligraphy, and we hung it on the bathroom door in the hospital room. I don't think either of us realized the significance of the placement at the time, but it was the most visible card in the room, and we began to live by the words written on it.

We reached a point where there was nothing else we could do other than trust that God, Travis' doctors, and the Department of Children's Services team were for us and our babies. I quit obsessively note-taking and making calls and sending emails, and just devoted my energy to prayer and supporting Travis in whatever ways he needed.

Don't get me wrong. I don't believe we should stay in our prayer closets without getting up and working, doing the things we can do to be the answer to someone's prayers, to effect positive change in the world, to bring glory to God, and to advance His Kingdom, but I do believe there comes a time in our lives and in certain seasons when we have done everything in our power, and we must open our hands and trust God with the thing. It can be hard to figure out when we've reached that point, but at this particular time it was not hard. I knew for certain I had to open my hands, relax, and quit white-knuckling the situation and give God the control that He had always deserved.

***

Scans, scans, everywhere scans. Most of those first few days are a blur. Scans are an interesting experience. I've never been scared of tight spaces. As a boy I would squeeze myself in behind the living room couches and fall asleep or read a book. That aspect of the scans didn't bother me. What bothered me about the scans was how cold the waiting areas were. I've never been cold natured. I've always "put the heat out" as my wife says referring to my high temperatures. To which I had often responded with thankfulness for stating the obvious that I'm very attractive. She would then slide her freezing ice-cube-toes under me to warm them up.

One of the first symptoms I remember is not being able to get warm. I was no longer a nuclear reactor of heat but a freezing leukemia patient. I couldn't get warm enough as I sat there waiting on my torso scan. Eventually I would learn to pile on the quilts for any trip downstairs. During one of those initial scans, I was given the option of listening to music. When given the options of genres, I chose outlaw country. If Waylon, Willie and Cash couldn't warm me up then no one could. I never got offered music again. Maybe it was the loud singing? I can't be held accountable for belting out those tunes. You can't give me the Highway Men and expect anything less. This won't be the last time Johnny Cash would be there for me.

For whatever reason I don't remember having a lot of "scanxiety" until the scan of my brain a day or two into our stay. Somehow, I had worked through my worries in other areas, but I was consumed with the condition of my brain. I'm a teacher, coach and preacher. I rely on my mind to feed my family. When contemplating the loss of brain function my entire body would begin to rattle uncontrollably. Of course, it would be one of the last scans in my initial admittance.

CHAPTER 13

Room 1751

W hen we made it to morning and the sun finally came streaming through the window, I felt like it had been the longest, darkest night of my life. I'm thankful that Travis has very little recollection of that night. I was worried about him, and I couldn't wait to see the sunrise. For some reason, I just felt like light would make all of it easier. Dr. Diaz was there very early in the morning, before his office hours began for the day. His face looked more peaceful than it had the night before. He was cheerier, and less rushed. He delivered good news. Travis' white blood cell count had already begun to drop after the first dose of ATRA through the night. Before he left for the office, he told us he would be back that night and that as soon as a room was available in the new Madison Street Tower the nurses would be moving us over there. The rooms were much larger on that wing of the seventh floor, and he wanted to make sure we were comfortable since we would be staying for a long time.

Dr. Diaz returned to the hospital room on Wednesday evening, night two of the long stay. He brought more good news from the battery of tests, biopsies, and scans that had been done throughout the day. He said all the scans that had been done so far looked good with no internal bleeding, and that the biopsy done under guided radiology did in fact, show that Travis had Acute Promyelocytic Leukemia, the one he had expected. When Dr. Diaz entered the room, I was sitting on the "window seat bed" that Doris and I had attempted to sleep on the night before. I noticed Travis immediately began to tremble. He knew this was the moment he would find out what his prognosis really looked like, and what the plan moving forward would be. I quickly got up from the window seat, and moved next to him on the hospital bed. I held his hand as Dr. Diaz delivered the news and the treatment plan. Doris was there and so were Kevin and Melissa. We all felt like the diagnosis was the best-case scenario if he had to have leukemia based on the information Dr. Diaz passed along, and we all felt like he was under the care of a great doctor who would make sure he had the best care.

***

I've recently rediscovered the importance of the word "together." I've lived the importance of the word all my life. As you've read it is easy to realize that we have a village of people who love us. I was born into a family where both of my parents had double digit siblings. One of the main reasons I married someone who didn't live in the Northwest Alabama area was because I had cousins everywhere. I know it is Alabama so it's okay—but it was not okay. As you can imagine, our family "get togethers" were major undertakings. From singing hymns to ring in the New Year to knock-down drag-out football games, we were together. With my diagnosis the togetherness amped up.

In Genesis 22, Abraham is given the command to sacrifice his covenantal son Isaac. When Abraham got close to the site of the sacrifice, he told his entourage to stay back while he and Isaac went to worship and then they would return. In verse six it says that Abraham and Isaac approached the site "together." The Hebrew word "yakh'-ad" means "unitedness." I don't believe in that instance it was just their geographical location, although that goes a long way. It was a singularity in purpose although they might not have exactly known how it would play out. It was an amazing feeling to have my wife there to hold my hand when any news came, good, bad or ugly. It meant even more that come what may, I wouldn't have to bear it alone. I'm the example of how "it is not good that man should be alone" (Genesis 2:18). I grew up singing the hymn, "Where No One Stands Alone" with tears in my eyes leading my home congregation, Jacksonburg Church of Christ in worship. I was finding out how much those words really meant.

***

A lot of people knew a very little bit about Travis' condition. Our whole school community was aware that Coach Creasy had leukemia. Thousands of people on social media knew that he had leukemia, but we hadn't put out any specific information at the time because we didn't have any specific information yet. We had been waiting on the piece of the puzzle that Dr. Diaz had just delivered. I asked to borrow Kevin's laptop, as I thoughtfully typed out a Facebook post for our friends and family to give them more insight into what we were facing, to ask them to pray, and to thank them for their kindness. The post said the following:

Dear Friends and Family,

Just 30 hours ago, I would never have believed that I would be so thankful for Travis' diagnosis of Acute Promyelocytic Leukemia. But here I am today, thanking God for a diagnosis of APL. The good news is it is considered the most curable form of adult leukemia with cure rates of up to 90%.

A little background, Travis pulled a muscle in his back about a month ago and began taking a steroid and muscle relaxer to help. About 10 days into the medication, he developed a huge black bruise on his side. He didn't even realize he had this bruise until I pointed it out. He came off the medication, but continued to bruise more easily than normal. Then over the last weekend, the bruising got a lot worse, and he began to have blood in his urine. He had some blood tests run at the doctor's office in Fayetteville on Monday and they referred him to a hematologist in Huntsville.

His appointment with Dr. Diaz (the hematologist/oncologist) was yesterday. I didn't even really understand that we were going to a cancer specialist. Dr. Diaz immediately told us that he believed Travis had leukemia, but a look at his blood cells under a microscope would confirm. He left the office, and came back and said it was definitely leukemia, and that they would do a bone marrow biopsy immediately and that he would be admitted to the hospital immediately afterward and that we should plan to stay for weeks rather than days.

This was a complete shock. I didn't have any idea this was what we were looking at when we went in. Dr. Diaz felt pretty positive from the beginning that his leukemia was APL based on the way he presented, but it took until tonight to confirm this.

The plan from here is that Travis will be in the hospital for the next 36ish days receiving chemotherapy and other therapies. After that, if his bone marrow biopsy shows no more leukemia cells, he will be allowed to go home, but we will continue to travel to Huntsville Monday-Friday for a 3-hour appointment that will include some infusions and molecular testing for another two months. The visits will then drop to one per week, then every other week and then once per month. The whole process will last for 6-8 months.

We have been so blessed by the outpouring of love from all of you. Thank you so much! So many of you have texted, called, sent messages, and visited. You have no idea how your prayers, company, and offers of help have blessed us. Our community of friends and family is amazing and we are so blessed. Thank you so much.

Travis enjoys having visitors, but starting tomorrow he will only be allowed to have 2 visitors at a time due to the chemotherapy he will be taking and the danger he will be in because of low immunity levels. If you want to visit, please come! Just understand we will have to cycle folks in and out 2 at a time. Also, if you're even a little sickly, please wait until you're feeling better. We don't want to risk any kind of infection. Again, thank you all so much. We love you all. We will do our best to keep you updated on how he is doing. Continue to pray. The treatment process will be long and hard on his body.

Grace & Peace,

Whitney & Travis Creasy

I was blown away at the responses. My phone was constantly lighting up with notifications from Facebook. I sometimes come down hard on social media, but it has its positives, and the networking capabilities for prayer needs ranks very high on the pro list. Every time I looked at my phone another person was offering their support through prayer. When I tell you those prayers carried us through the next few days and weeks, I mean we could feel a tangible warmth from these appeals to God on our behalf. I remember one day in particular, Travis woke up and said he had the best sleep he had since arriving at Huntsville Hospital. Later that day, as he was scrolling Facebook, he saw a message from a friend that said she woke up in the middle of the night thinking about him, and she didn't know what to pray so she just prayed that he would have a good night's rest.

Night two of the hospital stay wasn't nearly as dramatic as night one. The lights did actually go off in the hospital room, and there were fewer loud beeping alarms, and fortunately no nurses felt the need to run. Shortly after the brain scan, a nurse from the Madison Street Tower came to fetch us around 2:00 a.m. She was a cheery nurse with a bounce in her step, a big smile, sparkling eyes, curly hair, and the nurturing voice of a Kindergarten teacher. She told us there was a room ready for us over in the new Tower on the 7th floor and she would be moving us. I hopped up and began gathering our things; bags, clothes, pillow, blanket, snacks, books, etc... I carried a bunch of stuff and we piled a few things at the foot of Travis' hospital bed. Two nurses pushed him in that bed from the tiny room we had been in for a couple of days to his new home for the next five weeks, Room 1751.

We crossed the sky bridge that goes from the older wing of Huntsville Hospital to the newer Madison Street Tower. It was the first time I had noticed the Sky Bridge. It was a long, wide hallway with glass walls from the floor to the ceiling, so we had a view of the city in all directions. When we crossed the Sky Bridge, we came to a hallway that I had been to before. I recognized the nurse's station and the paintings on the walls. Travis and I had been here to visit Mrs. Jean Strope many years before. She was my basketball buddy, and so much more.

Her whole family, including her many grandchildren, attended church with us. She was a beautiful woman inside and out, and she loved her family fiercely. She enjoyed watching her grandkids play basketball so much she rarely missed a game even when she was very ill with ovarian cancer.

When I served as athletic director at RCA, I would sit with her in the bleachers for every basketball game. I rarely enter the gym at RCA during a varsity basketball game, even now—nine years after her death—without glancing at our spot in the bleachers and thinking about her. I felt a fluttering in my stomach like I would be sick when I thought about why I had been in this place before. As the nurses led us down the hall, we even entered a room on the same hallway that Mrs. Jean had stayed in when I came to visit her. I didn't remind Travis that we had been here before, I just wanted him to get some rest since he hadn't had much of an opportunity for it yet.

As the sun began to come up, the hallways of the hospital got a little busier. I heard someone outside the hospital room door, and realized that it was Dr. Diaz, there for his morning visit. He came in, looking a little defeated. He reported that the MRI of Travis' head showed that he had a small brain bleed. It was the first negative news we heard since starting treatment. Travis was scared. He was actually physically shaking again. *That* scared me. I couldn't help but wonder how bad it really was because I learned that Travis was obviously a lot tougher than I realized. He had let his health get to a point of almost no return before he even broke down enough to see a doctor about it.

I didn't have time to fret over it for very long before some nurses came and whisked Travis away for a CT scan of the spot on his brain. The scan confirmed that the bleed was old and that it was responding to treatment. A neurosurgeon came to visit a little while later, and she did a lot of mobility and strength tests to make sure Travis wasn't exhibiting any neurological symptoms. She said, "Dr. Diaz is on the right track treating this with the plan you're already on. This should heal just like all the bruises you can see on the outside of your body." Her words brought a flood of relief, and even though she was very kind and informative I hoped we would never see her again.

Later that morning, Cleo, Dr. Diaz's nurse practitioner came in to meet us. Cleo was a young woman with short dark hair and glasses. She was warm, energetic, friendly, and had a great smile. She reminded me a lot of my older cousin Amanda who is nurturing and fun. She confirmed something I had suspected since we had arrived at the hospital when she introduced herself.

"Hi, I'm Cleo. I'm Dr. Diaz's nurse practitioner here at the hospital. I usually do his rounds here, but I haven't been able to meet you yet because you've kind of been his pet. I'm here all day on normal workdays. You can find me anytime and ask any questions. I will be visiting with you at least once every day while you're here. We'll get to know each other well." I immediately liked her, and I knew her words were not just platitudes. She genuinely wanted to help if we had questions or concerns and she genuinely wanted to know her patients.

She would continue to advocate for Travis even after his hospital stay was over. I remember on Valentine's Day a few months later, Travis had terrible stomach pain and some nausea. He had already been having this pain for a while, and Dr. Diaz had ordered a scan of his abdomen. We had been to the main campus of CCI that morning for the scan before reporting to the Airport Road campus for his chemotherapy treatment. The intense pain started up that night after we got the kids in the bed. I ran to Walmart to buy Pepto Bismol, Gas-X, and every other over-the-counter medication I could find to see if that would help soothe his symptoms. Nothing seemed to work, so I called the CCI hotline for help. A familiar voice answered the phone, it was Cleo! She was on call that night, and she went above and beyond to help ease our minds and his symptoms. She looked at his scans from that day over the internet and told us there was nothing to be concerned about. She called in a prescription for Zofran to stop his nausea, and I was able to get it filled before the Walgreens pharmacy shut down for the night. She let Dr. Diaz know what was going on. Then, she texted me the next morning to ask how Travis was doing. She even told me to keep her cell phone number and call her if we ever needed her. I'm so thankful for all of the smart, loving, go-the-extra-mile kind of people that God put in our path. I was continually humbled by the care Travis received from the nurses, doctors, and technicians during the whole treatment process. I actually miss them sometimes. I don't miss the treatments or the hospital stay, but I did love the people God put in our path during that time. They were truly a blessing, and they made everything a little easier to deal with.

For the next 10 days or so, Travis was so much stronger than I ever expected him to be. A couple of oncology pharmacists came to see us soon after the neurosurgeon left. They told us all about his treatment protocol, the drugs they would be using, how they would be administered, their side effects, etc. They gave me a stack of information on each drug, to be honest I read some of the paperwork, but not all of it. I knew there were risks and scary side effects to all of the medications they were giving him, but I also knew that this treatment protocol had been tested and perfected for decades, and the disease was curable up to 90% of the time with it. I kept telling myself that I couldn't worry about the potential long-term side effects at the moment. I had to live in today, and continually be thankful for the answers we had for Travis' illness, the proven treatment methods, the capable and caring doctors and nurses, and our amazing support system of family and friends.

Staying in the present proved to be tough on some days. I continually reminded myself of Jesus' words in Matthew 6, "And which of you by being anxious can add a single hour to his lifespan?" (Matthew 6:27). The answer is none of us. But we can definitely take time *off* our lifespan with the stress we pile upon ourselves. Jesus gives some good advice that is full of grace for us as humans because he understands our plight here in this fallen world, "Do not be anxious about tomorrow, for tomorrow will be anxious for itself. Sufficient for the day is its own trouble" (Matthew 6:34). Jesus knows that we have the tendency to worry, and in this chapter of Matthew, he gives us permission to be concerned about what we have going on today.

There are seasons in life when we have to just stop and give over our worries and anxieties to Jesus every day; in fact, there have been times in my life when I had to stop and give them to Jesus every hour of every day, and the long hospital stay was one of those times. Sometimes it looked like going for a run in the sunshine and talking to God. Sometimes it looked like taking long deep breaths and reminding myself of all the small things God was taking care of, working out for our good; the "sparrow things" that he wasn't allowing to fall to the ground (Matthew 10:29). A lot of times it looked like singing along to Lauren Daigle's *Look Up Child* album and being reminded that He says, "I will send out an army to find you in the middle of the darkest night. It's true.

I will rescue you. I will never stop marching to reach you. In the middle of the hardest fight, it's true, I will rescue you."[1]

I guess the times my chest got the tightest, my breathing the shortest, and my body the shakiest was when I would think about the worst-case scenario. The one that I had been consumed with the night before Travis' diagnosis: the one where all the people I loved the most in the world were stripped away from me. The fear was still very real as Travis' four doses of his chemotherapy called idarubicin or "the Red Devil" began to catch up with him and as we still had no real answers for what would happen to our children after all this.

I made the dreaded phone call to the children's case manager on Thursday, October 18, the day after we found out Travis' confirmed diagnosis and his treatment plan. I had dreaded making this call since Travis and I had the conversation on Whitesburg Drive the night he was diagnosed. Our family members had rallied to help with the children for the next five weeks if DCS would work with us to make it happen, but I still felt like I was asking too much. I knew the arrangement would require a lot of extra leg work on behalf of the Children's Services case managers.

I walked out of Travis' hospital room and to the end of the long hallway and the massive window that looked northward over Huntsville and toward our home in Fayetteville. I sat down on the wide window seat and found the case manager's name in my contacts. I whispered a quick prayer before calling. I feel like all the words just came tumbling out when she answered. I'm not sure I paused for a breath. I probably sounded a little crazy, but I just wanted this conversation to be over with so I could remove it from the millions of other things swirling through my mind.

The case manager was gracious, and immediately offered her prayers for Travis, and told me that DCS would do anything in their power to keep the kids' placement from being disrupted! I was relieved to say the least. I had been in turmoil over the thought that we would lose them and not get a proper goodbye, and they would be left to figure out why they had been removed from yet another set of parents.

The social workers at DCS knew they were surrounded by a loving village where they felt safe and secure. I was so thankful God was watching out for us and for our babies throughout this time, but I still would wake up in the middle of night as I laid on my air mattress in the floor of Room 1751 at Huntsville Hospital in a cold sweat thinking about the possibility the kids could go home, and we wouldn't have our last days and weeks together as a family.

Again, I would have to give it over to Jesus. I would take several deep breaths and recount all the things I had to be thankful to God for handling. Doing this continually reminded me that God was working in ways I couldn't possibly see or understand yet. Like the fact that Travis didn't get sick while we were in Nashville. I was so thankful we made it through the weekend and got home to our doctor's office. As difficult as the diagnosis was, an ER visit far from home and family in Nashville would have been even tougher. And the fact that the hematologist/oncologist with an opening in his schedule in Huntsville on Tuesday, October 16 was Dr. Diaz; Travis could have landed with any doctor, but I was so thankful the doctor he "happened" to end up with was the smart, humble, cautious, and compassionate man that he was. I have so many examples of things that happened that paved the way for God's provision when we really needed it during the hospital stay.

I'm not sure when my heart began to believe that God could and would work things out for the good of our children as well. The whole experience actually makes me think of the story of Esther in the Bible. God is never mentioned in the story, but he is working the whole time behind the scenes even when the circumstances look the bleakest, like when Haman built gallows for Mordecai in his backyard (Esther 5:14). God revealed his hand, and the whole plot twisted, and Haman was hanged on the gallows he built for Mordecai (Esther 7:10). The Jews were saved from those who wanted to kill, destroy, and annihilate them (Esther 8). I slowly began to believe God was working in a way I couldn't see on behalf of the children. I had no evidence for it, but my heart earnestly expected a move of his hand at any moment because He was showing me over and over that he was providing for all our needs.

We made it through the 37 days with the kids staying at my mom's house for a few days, and then my grandparents and Travis' aunts, Mary and Edith, swapped in and out to keep the kids at our house. I will never forget Election Day in 2018. I left the hospital early that morning to go home to vote and visit with the kids. It was a gorgeous sunny and crisp Autumn day with beautiful leaves in every direction. I made it to my polling location soon after it opened, voted, and then went back home to see the kids.

I walked in the house, and it looked like the tornadoes that had swept through the Southeast the night before had made their way into our home! The kids were obviously running the show at 31 Hilltop Road. There were toys everywhere! When I say everywhere, I mean *everywhere*. I went to the bathroom and found one in the toilet. All the rules had gone out the window. Both kids knew we had a strict no eating in the living room policy, but there sat little Daniel in the middle of the living room eating his favorite snack, a granola bar. I got so tickled when I made my way to the kids' bedrooms. My grandmother had already bought both their own Christmas trees for their bedrooms, and Hailee had a TV, a Blu-ray player, and a new Christmas movie in her room! But the funniest part was that my grandmother said Hailee woke her up at 1:00 in the morning and asked her to make her scrambled eggs and grapes, and she obliged!

Before I went back to Huntsville, Daniel was on the lawnmower with his best buddy, "Dandaddy" blowing the carpet of yellow and orange leaves that had fallen in our front yard in a circle to be raked up. I realized that day that we would have two very spoiled toddlers on our hands when we finally made it home from the hospital.

***

On mid-term election day 2018, I of course was unable to vote because I'm a citizen of Tennessee and had not made provisions to vote from Huntsville Hospital. Honestly the last thing I wanted to think about was politics. Things have changed a good bit since 2018 to say the least but on that day, it was the farthest thing from my mind. That is until I got a DM on my twitter account from a former student named Alex. The DM read:

"I didn't like any of the senator candidates, so I wrote you in. You're in the race."

Now, the interesting thing is that I didn't think I had meant that much to Alex during his time at RCA. Maybe I still didn't but I thought his DM was pretty awesome.

***

We had a couple of phone conversations as a part of our daily routine in the hospital; one each morning and each night with my dad and one with the kids. My dad was faithful to call the hospital room's landline number early each morning around the time the doctor finished making his morning rounds and each night before bedtime. He learned all about the nighttime bloodwork routine and the markers that were indicators of improvement, and would ask what the doctor had to say about Travis' numbers each morning. Each night he would call back to ask how the day went, and if it looked like we would be home for Thanksgiving. He always asked me about Travis' mental state as well. He had spent a few days in the hospital a couple of years prior after having a heart attack, and he understood the anxiety that being couped up in a hospital room with a life-threatening health condition could induce. I appreciated those daily touchpoints with my dad a great deal during that time. I knew we were constantly at the top of his mind and his prayers during that season, and that was comforting.

We also talked to the kids every day on the phone or via FaceTime when the hospital WiFi would allow it, and they came to visit a handful of times. Those visits still stand out in Hailee's mind three years later. Occasionally, she asks me if

I remember when Nana brought her and Bubba to see Dada at the doctor. I tell her yes, I remember that. She usually doesn't have anything else to say. But sometimes she will say Dada was at the doctor for "like 100 days," 37 days, 100 days...I guess it's all the same in the mind of a three-year-old.

All the nurses at the hospital fell in love with the kids. They would ooh and aah over how cute they were. They were like little celebrities on the seventh-floor. There were times when nurses would literally come running out of the charting room or breakroom to see or talk to them. Come to think of it, I guess it is kind of rare to see toddlers on the cancer floor of a hospital. The first nurse to give Travis a dose of the "Red Devil" heard our whole foster care story because she had to spend 30 minutes face-to-face with him while she slowly pushed the cocktail into his veins. The kids were actually at the hospital for a visit when she came in to administer the dose. We all had to leave the room and go wait in the sitting room next to Travis' hospital room because children were not allowed to even be in the same room with the chemical. So, the nurse met the kiddos and Travis told her their story, our story, God's story while she pushed his medication. The next time she was in for work, she brought two gift bags to the room, one for each kid. The bags had coloring books, crayons, small toys, and Little Debbie cakes in them for the next time the kids came to visit.

Meanwhile, our family made sure the kids made it to their scheduled visitations, therapy sessions, and doctor appointments. I got a phone call from my mom one cold, rainy morning when she had dropped the kids off for a visit with their biological mom. She called me, and I could tell she was trying not to cry. The only thing she could get out of her mouth was, "I don't know how you do this." I knew the kids had a visit and that she must have just dropped them off. I was out running in a quaint little neighborhood adjacent to the hospital. I slowed my run to a walk to catch my breath so I could talk. I just told her I knew exactly what she was feeling. It is so very hard to leave the babies you love with someone and walk away knowing this someone could take them back soon.

ENDNOTES

[1] Daigle, Lauren. "Rescue." Track #2 on Look Up Child. Centricity Music, 2018, Compact Disc.

CHAPTER 14

Lucille & the Red Devil

D reary days in October just feel different now. It all "hits" different as my students say. I never really understood how the weather affected my mood until I had so much time on my hands to think about it. It's intimidating and a bit odd how some things are blurry and other things are crystal clear. I remember the rain falling as we entered CCI that first day, and the fresh air and rain I felt on my skin would be the last I'd feel until many days later following one of my scans on the first floor.

As they rolled me around the corner amid the chaos of the hospital, I noticed the sliding doors open to sweet freedom. The fresh air from outside hit me like a tidal wave; it wasn't like that first rainy day. There was so much Vitamin D to rejoice in. To dance in. For a moment I imagined I was running down the hallway with nurses chasing, my hospital gown flapping in the wind with a full moon working as a deterrent to anyone with hopes of stopping me. As many had done in the past, they would underestimate my speed and agility as I crossed the automatic door finish line. But, before I could make *a run for it the doors closed, and I snapped back to the reality; I had no shoes, and it was late autumn. At that point I might have taken my chances had we not already been on the elevator back to the seventh floor.*

The sky bridge on the seventh floor allows you to see the city, and despite much of the view being roof, it was still a nice view. One of the blessings of being locked down with the prettiest gal in the whole wide world is that you walk hand in hand with the prettiest gal in the whole wide world. We must have made that loop 100's of times together. As we made those trips around the hallway it was at best interesting and at worst difficult to see all those rooms occupied by other people dealing with cancer. Some of those patients never seemed to have one single visitor darken the door, but I was spoiled by my revolving door of friends, family, and brothers and sisters in Christ. It took all of that and more to keep the fight alive. It is painful to think of having to go at it alone. Many people do it and they impress me beyond measure. Of course, there are some who seem alone, but God is with them every step of the way.

Unfortunately, we always made the 7th Floor circle with a third wheel with four wheels of her own. "Lucille" was a pain in the backside. Lucille was my dance partner for the entirety of my hospital stay. We were inseparable. I'd pace the floor watching a football game; she'd pace right along with me. I'd lay in bed and she'd pump arsenic trioxide into my aorta, or she'd pump plasma into my veins. Lucille was the epitome of the adage, "can't live with her and can't live without her." She was my IV pole. I guess she wouldn't have been such a bad dance partner had I not had the best to compare her to, My Whitney. If I never see Lucille again it will be too soon.

To my knowledge, between my hospital stay and treatments at the clinic I've had over 80 infusions of arsenic trioxide. Yes, you read that first word correctly. Of course, it was highly "watered down" arsenic but it was arsenic, nonetheless. I was told that arsenic is at the very least "organic," and my unspoken response to that statement was, "So is snake venom!"

I remember when it actually hit me just how many infusions I'd had. I was reading an article about a young man who had received 60 chemotherapy infusions in 3 years. I was telling Whitney of his bravery when she responded "How many do you think you've had?" and I began to add them up. I think I had 86 arsenic trioxide infusions between October 2018 and March 2019. I had one every day of my hospital stay and then 5 days a week from just before Thanksgiving to early March.

Dr. Diaz was not kidding when he said they were going to hit me pretty hard. I literally trusted him with my life. Of course, God is ultimately in charge of my expiration date. Glad they worked so well together! When I was in the hospital, they used a PICC Line that was placed in my left arm and ran up into my armpit and into the aorta of my heart so that the medication could be dispersed through my body. I now understand why it was so important to keep my heart rate checked and keep it level.

To start my treatment, I was given 4 doses of "The Red Devil." As you can imagine that is not necessarily a vote of confidence. When the nurse who has to administer it through a "push" basically puts on a hazmat suit to deliver it, you know it's the "good stuff," meaning it is going to make you feel like trash.

So, for every other day for 9 days, a nurse would come into

my room and make everyone leave. Then slip on the "Kevlar" and sit face to face with me as they would slowly push the red devil into my PICC line over a half hour. You might imagine what the conversations were like being in close quarters like that. Talk of leukemia typically didn't last long as the minutes ticked by, we'd chat about family and to my wonderful surprise, God.

Makes me think of how Paul might have felt every time his Roman house arrest guard changed. "Someone new to share the Gospel with" or maybe it was someone from a few days prior so they could pick up where they left off. Maybe they weren't allowed to converse much.

In that room on the 7th floor of Huntsville Hospital, I was blessed to be cared for by some amazing human beings. One thing was for sure, for that 30 minutes every other day, I wanted that person to know that whatever the outcome was, God is awesome. I might not have said that every day but my walls were covered with well wishes from believers like you.

Once I finished my "running with the devil" treatment I switched over to the two-hour arsenic trioxide infusion. My "nurse of the day" would come in and go through the task of suiting up, asking me my name/birthdate and hang my IV bag on my trusty partner Lucille then they'd begin the drip. During my two-hour treatment, I would have to lay down to get as comfortable as possible with a tube running out of my arm and poison making its way into my aorta. I could feel my body heat rising and my energy leaving my body.

On Saturdays there were football games to watch. I attempted to watch Alabama beat Tennessee, but it was too much orange. On days when there was no football, I tried to watch movies. We started with boxing movies. I watched "Cin-

derella Man" one day and "Rocky" the next. Rocky is a movie that has a tremendous influence on my life. My dad is a big Sylvester Stallone fan. I can remember watching Sly in everything from "Cobra" to "Over The Top," but growing up, I disliked the first "Rocky" movie. Hope I'm not ruining it for you but he loses. As a kid I much preferred Rocky IV because he whoops Drago and gets revenge for his friend's death. Classic 80's story.

As I've grown older, the first movie has become my favorite. I don't know how old I was exactly when I found tears rolling down my face when Balboa returned home from the arena the night before the fight. He admits to Adrian that he can't beat Apollo. He follows that admission up with that he just wants to go the distance because no one had ever gone the distance with Apollo Creed. He wanted to go every round of the fight and be standing at the end. That had a profound meaning for me prior to this dark time, but even more so now. I didn't know the ending but I wanted to finish what the LORD had started in me.

Unfortunately, I had to switch from the exciting sports movies to something a little less intense because they caused my heart rate to climb which is a big "no-no" when your heart is pumping harmful stuff throughout your body. So "The Office" took over before we could get to the next installment of the Rocky saga "Rocky Balboa." There is a scene in that movie where Rocky's son confronts the aging former boxer about the large shadow he has cast on his life. Rocky responds with some very important words that have impacted me greatly before and after this episode in my life.

The world ain't all sunshine and rainbows. It's a very mean and nasty place and I don't care how tough you are. It will beat you to your knees and keep you there permanently if you let it. You, me, or nobody is gonna hit as hard as life. But it ain't about how hard ya hit. It's about how hard you can get hit and keep moving forward. That's how winning is done! Now if you know what you're worth then go out and get what you're worth. But ya gotta be willing to take the hits, and not pointing fingers saying you ain't where you wanna be because of him, or her, or anybody! Cowards do that and that ain't you![1]

It feels like I've deeply received this message throughout my life when I needed it most whether it was through coaches, experiences, or the Scriptures. Jesus put it more succinctly, "But the one who endures to the end will be saved" Matthew 24:13, NIV). I feel like I've had conversations similar to the one above with the Almighty and his answer seems to be consistent. All I could get through were light hearted tv shows. My mental capacity just couldn't handle anything heavy. In fact, it is 2021 and I'm just now getting back to where I can handle a heavier movie or television show. These infusions were certainly an area where my refusal to ask a lot of nosey questions helped me. I didn't really want to know what the ramifications were. I just knew it was something that had to be done to blast my immune system and teach it a lesson. Hopefully a lifelong lesson. One of my nurses used the illustration of my white count being a frat boy who had gotten out of control and needed to be reined back in.

The whole experience was a roller coaster of emotions. I

had control of my thoughts and emotions for a moment. Then out of nowhere I was mad and frustrated. At some point prior to my diagnosis, I had gotten the newest Spider-Man video game. Here I was with a marathon of days in the hospital and a Playstation 4 and one of my favorite heroes at my disposal. Every time I tried to play, I would get so frustrated with the first level. The first and usually easiest level. I had zero fortitude to carry on because I could feel my body heat rise and my uncontrolled anger getting more difficult to contain. So, I quit and may have tried once or twice more. After getting back home, I went back to play it and finished the first level in fifteen minutes. It was mind boggling just how zapped I was but I was regaining my strength every day. The Gospel of John records some of the background to the Life of Jesus in almost a theatrical way. He mentions that it was dark during the Last Supper as Judas leaves. We believe that John was the youngest Apostle according to Jewish tradition that the youngest person at the Passover meal gets to ask the questions. It must have been difficult for Peter to allow John to be the spokesman since Peter seemed to fill that role unofficially. It is a vivid picture to me because little Hailee always wants her opinion to be heard but Daniel often gets the attention which makes her all the more antsy. Forgive me if I envision Peter and John similarly. I bring up that scene of the Seder because it seems that it ends with more questions than answers especially for those who were present that night. Cancer treatment often feels similar. Every treatment or update leads to more questions. Another reason I'm thankful that Whitney was there to ask all the questions that I couldn't think to ask. In a very real sense during my hospital stay and five-day-a-week treatments that followed behind were a "glass case of emotion." From the nicknames of the treatments, to the scanxiety, to the survivor's guilt, you never know where your mind would lead.

RCA won the right games to make the 2018 MTAC Bowl. Our final record was three wins and seven losses. I was unable to Coach the last two games due to my diagnosis. The Friday after my diagnosis the team would travel up to Bowling Green, Kentucky to play against Coach Don Brown's Warriors of Bowling Green Christian Academy. The game was rainy and messy. As you can imagine the Knights were not up to playing with the heaviness of the situation but my presence would not have changed anything as BGCA was a great team that year. I was unable to listen or watch the game so it was the first game I hadn't coached the Knights in eleven years. Due to BGCA being the higher seed they were set to host us again the following Saturday for the MTAC Bowl. Coach Brown will always have my gratitude because of his willingness to relocate the game to Fayetteville in an act of tremendous respect and sportsmanship.

I was able to call the team from the hospital room that Championship Saturday. We did not use the facetime call as I'm sure I didn't look that great. They also played an audio only version of a video "pep talk" on the stadium PA prior to the game. I rewatched that video again recently and it was a strong reminder of how tired I was. I watched the game as much as I was able through the 8 Man Extreme YouTube stream but my blood pressure got too high, so I had to cut it off. The boys put up a fight that day but it wasn't enough as Bowling Green won. I made sure to call Coach Brown to thank him for the relocation and congratulate him on the win.

Not being able to coach those last two games for our lone Senior, running back John Trahin, added extra motivation to *get back on the sideline for the class of 2020. Our theme for the 2018 season was "FINISH" and that would continue through the rest of my treatments. You might call it stubborn, and depending on the day I might agree, but I hope it is leaning more toward resolve.*

At some point, I began running a fever and broke out in hives. I was highly uncomfortable especially from the starched hospital gown rubbing against the small little red bumps covering most of my body. I remember getting very perturbed with a nurse who had come in during the middle of the night to take my blood pressure. The cuff that went around my arm was irritating on a good day. It was the middle of the night, I had hives, a fever, and I was on some sleep aid that did not make the circumstances better. I asked her as nicely as I could muster in the situation if I could take the cuff off. She was not able to grant my request as it was of utmost importance to keep a monitor on my heart because we were after all pumping arsenic trioxide to it. I remember speaking with her very disrespectfully. The next day I told Whitney that I wish I had not been that ill with her. She assured me that it was understandable. Still, it was not her fault that I was in this particular set of circumstances.

The fever and hives were the symptoms of a greater problem. A problem that could only be solved by an infectious disease doctor. An appointment was made for us to meet or at least for him to come to my home on the seventh floor. When he entered the room, I could tell he was fairly nervous about the encounter.

I can't begin to imagine the stress involved in keeping a hospital protected from infectious diseases and that is before even considering the potential hazards to immune deprived human beings. I'm sure he was not the only one involved in this effort. He entered my room and began to speak with a thick accent but I was able to understand him. He looked like Sacha Baron Cohen's character "Jean Girard" from "Talladega Nights: The Ballad of Ricky Bobby," and sounded like him too. It would've been difficult to take him seriously if not for the direness of the situation. He was not kidding around and thankfully so, although I prefer things to be lighthearted.

Up until that point I thought I had a very small personal bubble—if any at all—this guy discovered it; and this guy popped it. For some reason, he pushed every uncomfortable button I had just by being in my presence. Looking back, it had more to do with the fact I had been poked and prodded enough. He hadn't even done his worst yet and I was annoyed. He ordered a battery of tests. I was beginning to get accustomed to hearing the word "tests." Although at that point I would've gladly accepted a math test instead of the examination he meant. What he meant were several blood tests and a stool sample. Yes, a stool sample. I was intrigued as to how this would occur. My mind raced between the worst and best possible scenarios for acquiring this sample.

Later in the day, a nurse brought a clear container that looked like an upside down "ten-gallon" cowboy hat. The brim went between the seat and toilet, allowing the top to catch the sample. The instruction was to push the call button attached to my bed when the sample was ready. Notice there was no mention of how much of a sample was necessary.

I'll take a minute here to inform you that you cannot underestimate or predict the impact chemo has on various body systems; the bowels are no different. I had learned to distrust my body and this is still somewhat of a struggle to this day. I never really knew when I'd need to go again. I remained on softener well after I left the hospital all the way to the end of my oral chemotherapy. So, when it was "go time" in the middle of the night, it was "go time!"

As I have mentioned, going anywhere in the hospital is difficult due to your attachments such as my dancing partner Lucille. At this particular time, I had woken from a deep sleep. So, I was forced to maneuver Lucille around my wife and mom who were sleeping on the floor all while hastily trying to get to the bathroom. I made it, but barely. The thought hit me that they didn't necessarily mention how much they needed. The container they provided was huge. I concluded that I needed to go for the gusto. I certainly didn't want to have to do it again. I filled it to capacity and walked out of the bathroom back into the living area of my room. Everyone was awake as often happened when I got out of the bed suddenly in the middle of the night. Another reason I wasn't keen on getting up that much. I know it always alarmed mom and Whitney.

I felt like I walked out there with a smug and accomplished look on my face. I smashed the call button and patiently waited for them to arrive. When the nurse arrived, he revealed a small ice cream scoop shaped utensil. I quickly realized that I had done too much. As he walked by me, I apologized to him and he responded that it wasn't that big of a deal. Apparently, he does that a lot. He walked out with his sample and I went back to sleep. The hives and fever continued for a few days as they worked through the different tests. One day I woke up to an awesome treat as I watched the RCA faculty and staff perform a lip sync and choreograph routine on Facebook. Most of the act was hilarious but at some point, it turned emotional. As I began to cry the infectious disease doctor returned. It was terrible timing as I certainly didn't want him thinking something else was afflicting me and set off more testing. I explained to him the situation, and that everything was fine.

The tests revealed the hives were a reaction to an antibiotic I had been receiving high doses of since arriving at the hospital. It was a good thing that it was only the high doses of it that caused the reaction because they accidentally gave me another dose within days of that revelation. I remember the distraught look on the nurse's face when she had to inform me of the mixup. We assured her that there were no hard feelings and, on that occasion, since it wasn't a high dose, I had no reaction.

During my time dealing with the hives, people began to bring me amazing gifts. I received many robes to lounge around in. I had two especially soft robes. One blue and one crimson. Occasionally, I still will put those on and enjoy the great comfort they brought me. Just like the hospital gown, the sheets were starched to help with disease, so they were especially itchy to sleep on with the breakout. Someone brought me plush comforters, and my rest was much improved.

My hair began to fall out a little at a time. I never lost clumps of hair like so many others do. My hair just became an annoyance as I woke up with it all over me even after bathing every night before bed. Eventually Whitney's grandmother Ann came and buzzed my hair really short. I never lost all my hair and for that I'm very grateful.

As an extrovert, it was difficult to think about all the awesome activities I was missing out on. For the most part I want to be out doing all the fun things of life. I knew I would drive myself mad staring at the four walls of that room. I had to get intentional about my time. I needed to use it wisely.

Depending on your circumstances, 15 minutes can seem like a long time. Depending on your age, 15 minutes can feel very short. I would experience both in a half hour span throughout the day. I'd start my day off listening to entire albums of Lauren Daigle or Johnny Cash followed by reading a chapter of several different books. By 9 AM I was onto word puzzles. Then I'd begin to receive visitors. Oh, how wonderful it was to get visitors! I'd stay pretty busy until my treatment in the afternoon/evening knocked me on my back. After that I might watch the crane worker build the parking deck right outside my window. I owe that person a lot of money for the entertainment he provided. Then the worst would happen, the sun would go down.

On one hand the days seemed so short but on the other, the nights felt like they dragged on and on. It was at night I developed the "next 15 minutes" method. I'd pray to God to get me through the next 15 minutes and then we'd talk again. After a while, that method crept into the daylight hours as well. There's only so much you can do on the 7th floor of Huntsville Hospital; and if you went to any other floor, it was for a scan so the dreaded scanxiety was around every corner down there. There were certainly 15 minutes that were easier to get through and some not so much; but because of God, I did get through it. I challenge you to use each minute wisely because they do add up. I'm heading into several years since my diagnosis and sometimes it's hard to even remember those days. As difficult as they were, I don't know that I've ever had a more in-depth relationship with God.

One of the hardest days of my Huntsville Hospital "visit" was October 31, 2018. Yes, Halloween was a hard day. As stated previously I really like events. I'm always ready for the

next fun opportunity. I was already missing my kids something fierce. It seemed like they were growing a foot every few
days. I was missing so many things that I would never get
back. In normal circumstances I suffer from FOMO, the "fear
of missing out." But there I was stuck in the hospital, and they
were going to get dressed up and go trick-or-treating. It was
brutal and only added to the recurring thought that I was
never going to see and experience the outside again. Couple my
longing to leave those four walls with the complete lack of
interest in eating and we had a problem. I had no desire to eat
anything because it was like gnawing on tinfoil. One of the
nurses suggested I drink "Ensure" because it was a quick way to
get nutrients without the "drudgery" of eating.

I had a familiarity with the drink because my older
brother Bradley had a feeding tube placed because he had a
tendency to get dehydrated and also had trouble swallowing. It
was always a bit bizarre to me when they would give him the
Ensure that he would lick his lips like he could taste it. Of
course, in my curiosity I had tasted it a time or two. It wasn't
bad at all. In those instances, they gave it to him pretty quick.
So, I thought nothing of it and proceeded to down one of them
in short order at lunch. When they wheeled around dinner, I
told them to bring me another Ensure. I chugged it as well.

That's when the third worst stomach pain I've experienced
struck. The pain when you're worried about sitting up because
you are going to spew all the elements contained in your body.
Then the visitors began to pour into the room. It's the first clear
memory of just wanting to lay there in my stupidity and throw
the biggest pity party I could organize with my limited
resources. From my belly button to my throat, I was feeling like
death. My mind was focused on all the things I'd rather be

doing featuring Hailee and Daniel. Our dear friend Debbie Cooper sent Whitney pictures of the kiddos in their Halloween outfits and all I wanted to do was cry. It was a helpless feeling. I so desperately wanted to be the life of the party but I couldn't find a reason to be my normal self. I wasn't my normal self, and there was no way of hiding it.

I remember being told later that the amazing Mrs. Krysa Spears who was in the hospital room that night was pretty upset by the way I acted. I'm reminded of Jesus' great promise in the Beatitudes of Matthew that "Blessed are those who mourn because they'll be comforted." I was too stubborn to be comforted. I literally had three mommas in the room that would've gladly comforted me and I refused to break down and accept it. I'm sure it was awkward because of my denial. Unfortunately, it wasn't the first time, nor it will be the last time I was too stubborn.

ENDNOTES

[1] Rocky Balboa, Director Sylvester Stallone (Las Vegas, Los Angeles, Philadelphia: MGM Distribution Co./Sony Pictures Releasing, 2006).

CHAPTER 15
Going Home

Ituations seemed like everyone we crossed paths with became personally invested in our story during that time, and it was like God in his kindness placed each of them along our road to lift us up and encourage us at just the right moment. Most days, Travis had several visitors pop in and out. Many of them were his football players or former players. One night, two of my favorite Knights dropped by together, Austin Wooten and Josh Brooks. I love those boys, well I guess they're men now, but I will always think of them as two of my boys. My mom and stepdad Jody were there at the time too. Just before Josh and Austin got ready to leave, Austin pulled his 2013 football championship ring out of the front pocket of his Carhartt overalls and gave a speech about what Travis meant to him and what the sport of football had meant to him. His eyes were teary; he had already lost his mother to cancer as a young teenager. When he was finished, he asked Josh to pray. My heart could have exploded with thankfulness to God for the good and perfect gift of our relationship with these young men. When they left, Jody marveled at Austin's honesty, vulnerability, and bravery.

The days and weeks went on, and we missed the kiddos and counted down until we could all be back together again—we hoped it would be on Thanksgiving Day! The weekend before Travis was set to go home, I went and picked the kiddos up from daycare. They were excited to see me pick them up, and I told them we were going to go buy Daddy some new tennis shoes before we went home. We realized he had no shoes to wear outside once they let him go because the shoes that he arrived in were thrown away because they were soaked in his blood from the bone marrow biopsy. He had been wearing a pair of house shoes that my grandmother brought him since then.

At our local Hibbett Sports, I got both toddlers out of their car seats and bundled them in their coats to ward off the bitter cold. We made our way in, Hailee holding my left hand and Daniel perched on my right hip. I told the kids they could pick Daddy's shoes out. Hailee immediately went for a bright red pair of Air Jordans! I should have known she would go for the swaggiest, most expensive pair of shoes in the joint. I talked her into a pair of dark green Adidas tennis shoes because they were Travis' favorite color. She seemed happy with that, and we purchased the shoes then headed to McDonald's for Happy Meals.

Travis' aunt Myra and her sister-in-law Brenda stayed with the kids that weekend, so they met us at home. I stayed and took care of the bedtime routine that night before heading back to the hospital. Hailee was not ready for me to go, but I assured her that there were only a few more days left before Daddy could come home, and that she was coming to visit with him the next day.

The few times the kids visited Travis in the hospital, he was very emotional. We walked the hallways together and looked out over the city on the sky bridge. The kids loved pushing the buttons that opened the doors for wheelchairs and the ones in the elevator. The visits obviously made an impression on Hailee too. She remembers something about that time, because there is a picture of her that was taken at daycare on one of the days my mom picked them up and brought them to visit. Every time she sees that picture, she talks about how that was the day she came to the "doctor" to see dada when he stayed there for "a long week."

***

The sun rose on the day that I truly believed would never come. I was going home not a moment too soon. Or was it? The day I had counted down to but also lost track of was finally here. It was an odd feeling of euphoria to go home but also anxiety about leaving the friendly confines of Huntsville Hospital with basically a new immune system. I had never been a germaphobe in my life. Prior to Leukemia, I was a firm believer in the 5 second rule and grossing people out by eating/drinking after them. It was well known that if you wanted to keep your food or drink do not leave it sitting around where it might find its way into my hands. That guy went the way of the Doh-Doh Bird. Now I was stepping back out into the wild. I couldn't wait to feel the cool November air but was concerned about my infant immune system.

My last day started with a trip down to what seemed like

the basement of the hospital. I had several not-so-fun things to do before making my way back to Fayetteville. The events on my final day itinerary were another biopsy and a spinal tap. This was certainly something I was hoping to avoid but alas there I was in the bowels of Huntsville Hospital waiting to be poked and prodded. A tradition at this point.

I was in the bed with Whitney sitting by my side as the Doctor strolled through the curtain that provided us with some privacy. The doctor was a young guy with blonde wavy hair past his ears. As he began to speak, he kind of stumbles, knocking around some things on the tray beside my bed and dropping his pen. As he bends to pick up his pen he says, "I can't do anything right today." As you can imagine this does not instill a lot of confidence. It was very difficult to not demand him go outside the curtain and start over.

As they rolled me down the hallway to the room where the spinal tap would be administered, I remember thinking the area looked like the location where all the hardcore matches occurred during the 1990's pro wrestling episodes. I kept waiting for "Mankind" with his brown mangled mask and maniacal matching jumpsuit to jump out from behind one of the columns and try to hit me with a chair or a random baseball bat wrapped in barbed wire. Mankind was a character who was basically a mental patient that lived in the boiler room of whatever arena Vince McMahon's crew was performing. I was stunned when they wheeled me into a room that had pipes running all over the ceiling and walls. The only relief I felt was in my comparison of Mankind to the clumsy doctor; it was an upgrade.

As is the case for any procedure, it takes a while to get set up so there is time for small talk. The person assisting had defeated breast cancer and we were swapping "war stories" as the doctor rolled up in his stool and began to explain the process. They were going to draw some spinal fluid to run some tests (there is the word again) to make sure the leukemia had not spread to my spine. Some of the fluid would be mixed with chemotherapy and shot back into my spine. To make sure they were where they needed to be along my spinal column he would "tap" a certain spot. If my leg jumped and a warm sensation like I was peeing made its way down my leg he had hit the right spot. I was laying on my stomach so at least I didn't have to watch—or so I thought. Right in front of my face was a shiny metallic door knob shaped attachment to one of the pipes. I couldn't make out all the details but enough that I could see what was going on. It was like I could not look away even though everything in me was screaming to hide my eyes. It was too late. He tapped one spot. His "can't do anything right" streak continued. He had missed. Thankfully he got it the second time. There I was in Mankind's boiler room with two complete strangers while I felt like I was peeing my pants. Thank God for pain blockers! I don't know if I had just been poked and prodded so much that I was numb or the doc actually got two things right. Whatever it was, I'm grateful for it.

One of the last events before leaving the hospital was the removal of my PICC line from inside my left bicep. I didn't realize how long that tube was but it ran up into my armpit and directly into my aorta so the arsenic trioxide and idarubicin could be distributed through the rest of my body. It still gives me the creeps thinking that some level of arsenic was pumped right into my heart. I thought for sure this would require another trip downstairs but two nurses came and separated me from my closest frenemy. They put on their chemical glasses and had me turn my head away from them to protect me from the buildup or residue inside the tube. You know the stuff they'd pumped into my heart the last thirty plus days!

It wasn't long before I was in a wheelchair and headed for the rotating door out to my wife who was waiting for me in the Armada to go home. HOME. A place at times I thought I might not ever see again. At other times I thought it was a fantasy land that wasn't real: a place that housed my kids, my own bed and my dog, a wonderful door, a roof that is my favorite color and trees that I'd curse every fall when the leaves dropped. It was too good to be true. I was finally going home. I remember hitting the parkway on 431 North out of Huntsville and looking back at my temporary home for the last month or so. The feeling of triumph was quickly fading to the question of "Am I ready?" Was my immune system ready? The initial battle was over but what was to come? This would never be over, with a tear in my eye, I mustered up enough courage to look north up that familiar highway. We passed Alabama A&M, then into Meridianville. As we entered Hazel Green, I laughed to myself about how often I'd remarked the irony that Hazel Green High School's main color isn't actually green. I'd never really cared for the scenery of Hazel Green, but it sure was beautiful that night! Victory looked good on Hazel Green —the last town in Alabama before crossing the state line—but victory looked even better from my house on Park City Hill in Fayetteville, Tennessee!

As we pulled into our driveway, there were a few members of our church family there to greet and cheer for us. I sat in the car for what felt like several hours but was only for a few seconds. It was one of the few times in my life I didn't know what to say. I was scared to celebrate too much; I was scared to say much of anything to anyone. I felt like a zombie staggering out of the car down the walk way to our front door. If I said anything to anyone it wasn't much. The last thing I recall was my head hitting the pillow in my own glorious bed.

In the hospital, contact with anyone was limited due to my weakened immune system, so Whitney and I were limited to hand holding, a few hugs, and even less kisses. This may come as a shock to many of you but we are cuddlers at the Creasy household. It has only become "worse" since those long days on the seventh floor. There are very few places that rival the couch with us all huddled up and piled on. It certainly doesn't hurt our golden retriever's feelings either.

***

Dr. Diaz has been everything and more than we could have asked for in an oncologist. He explains things in ways that are easy to understand, he is patient with my research and loads of questions. He is extremely cautious and always has Travis' best interest at heart, he is not afraid to seek a second medical opinion, and he is kind, has a great bedside manner, and one of the warmest smiles I have ever seen. Travis' second phase of treatment took place at the CCI offices in Huntsville under Dr. Diaz and a host of oncology nurses' care. We felt confident that Travis was receiving the best care possible.

***

When I got out of the hospital, I began the 2-hour arsenic trioxide treatments five days a week. Due to my class schedule and freedom to arrange my treatments I was able to go back to work which was a wonderful feeling. I truly live the Mark Twain ideal of find a job you enjoy doing, and you will never have to work a day in your life. Riverside was such a blessing to me throughout my treatment. They were an amazing support group of loyal Christians, many of whom helped transport me to and from CCI in Huntsville.

I would teach my classes until midday, get in the car with my chauffeur for the day and drive south 30-45 minutes every work day. I'd go up to the 4th floor of CCI and check in. Checking in involved checking my heart rate and making sure my body would be able to handle the arsenic trioxide for the day. Then I would be called back to the infusion room where all of the angelic nurses presided over people of all ages who had been stricken with the dreaded "C word" and other blood related illnesses. Depending on what day of the week and time determined who my Cancer ward buddies were. Sometimes the people who sat near me were talkative and wanted to share their struggles, others never uttered a word. Some were more compliant with the nurse's advice and others were openly defiant. I once heard a discussion between a nurse and an older gentleman that involved the nurse asking if the gentleman had drunk enough liquids the night before. His response of "Yes, I drank coffee and beer" was humorous but of course that is not what she meant. She rephrased and asked specifically about how much water intake he had consumed as she reminded him that coffee and beer actually dehydrate. He said that he had not drank water and wasn't going to change that. The nurse made one more attempt and then turned to assist someone else.

On one occasion I entered the chemotherapy treatment

area and sat by a gentleman who overheard how long I would be there on that specific day. He stated his jealousy and how he would like to only have to stay for a couple of hours every week or couple of weeks. When I informed him that I had that treatment every workday he said he would rather stick with his current schedule. He was a jolly fellow all things considered and we struck up a friendship. It is always difficult to judge someone's age when diagnosed with cancer because of the toll it takes on the body, so my best guess is he was in his fifties. He may have been younger but going through chemo and radiation will age anyone. He's a veteran who was diagnosed with tongue Cancer and I vaguely remember him mentioning that he'd had at least two bouts with the disease. At this point in his treatment, they had removed a portion of his tongue but it didn't impede our lively discussions. Because he was there several hours, he always had a backpack full of snacks. I mentioned that I enjoyed Reese's Cups and beef jerky. I believe he came ready with those two items every time he came to CCI just in case we got to enjoy one another's company.

Always steadfast during my treatments were the nurses. The CCI nurses are awesome. From the first person who took my blood to the last person who took it just a few months ago, they have been nothing but professional and kind. It might be kind of odd, but I miss my infusion nurses at the Crestwood campus. Unfortunately, I don't get to see them at all due to the Covid protocols, otherwise, I would occasionally pop in and let them see how I was doing. You certainly develop favorites and in the category of taking my blood the two ladies who work at the Crestwood office are the best. I very rarely even felt a sting when they took my blood. Their office is always adorned with Scriptures and statements of faith. They brought such comfort *to me when I was there. My infusion nurses were very informative. On the first day we were introduced to a folder full of information about do's and don'ts of chemotherapy treatment. These included eating to bathroom habits. I'm glad Whitney was there with me so I didn't have to remember it all.*

After check-in and avoiding being called back to accounting, I'd watch the fish swim around in their tank. I'm not sure who kept them fed and alive but I thank them. There were several large goldfish swimming around and watching them was relaxing. Whitney did not enjoy sitting in the lobby because of the "cancer commercials" that ran across the flatscreen mounted on the wall. The fish tank was embedded into the wall back in the corner in an "L' shape to the right just past the flat screen mounted on the wall as you come into the lobby. If you were sitting near the fish tank you couldn't see the tv with its cancer infomercials and I believe that is why that corner was so popular. Just about every seat was filled over there.

Once my name was called, I went back through the door and continued down the hall to the room on the right where vitals were taken. This was the same room where I watched the older gentleman ring the bell the day I was diagnosed. It was a room with two seats on opposite walls with fold-down armrests so they could collect blood pressure and other important data. In the middle of the room was a scale. For some reason I took a lot of determination from that scale. If I was under 155 pounds and I was most of the time, I'd use that to push me to keep fighting. From the vitals room, I'd visit the blood drawing ladies who were always efficient (You ladies are the real MVPs!). That room was closer to the lobby down the hall and to the left. The blood draw room had two chairs facing the hallway with a window to an office between them. The chairs were like the ones found in the vitals room with the fold-down arms for better "lead checking" angles. The ladies would draw about three vials worth every trip. After that it was back to the lobby to wait for my rat poison cocktail to be created for disciplining my white blood cells. Once that had been accomplished, the nurse who would be my attendee for the day came to the door in the lobby and took me back.

The infusion room was back down the old familiar hallway and directly across from the vitals room. As you enter on the left is another scale and on the right is that glorious bell. The glorious bell that everyone who walks, crawls and drags themselves through that opening hopes to one day ring. It's shiny little smirk and tightly woven rope hang ready to be rung off the wall.

From the bell, there are 3 horseshoe-shaped groups of the most comfortable chairs available. They lay back and have seat warmers. If it wasn't enough to keep us warm, there were machines on the right side of the room that kept stacks and stacks of blankets warm. Also, there were wonderful volunteers who kept me stocked up on snacks from peanut butter crackers to hot chocolate! The whole setup was to help us relax and forget why we were there. The atmosphere was great. On some occasions, chaplains would come in and have a small devotional period. They were always so chipper that I think they might've gotten on some nerves from time to time. I was always glad to see them as they added some excitement to the room. When I think back on it, I realize what a tough job that would've been. To come into a room of people, most of which are fighting for their lives and some who felt they were losing and try to minister, that had to be difficult.

I'm sure things have changed now concerning visitors because of COVID, but when I was taking treatments, we were allowed to have one adult visitor sit with us. Although most of my drivers offered to sit in there with me, I never asked them to. I could think of 1,000 other places I'd rather be, so I certainly wasn't going to insist on them staying. I usually passed my time between the book "Team of Rivals" about Abraham Lincoln, editing the 2018 Varsity Football highlight reel, and playing a card game on the provided iPads attached to the walls between the treatment chairs. One time I did have a neat Civil War magazine that Krysa Spears had bought for me. As I was looking at the magazine an older gentleman asked me about it and so I let him look through it. He seemed intrigued. His eyes told the story of his interest. He looked a lot like Colonel Sanders with his white lightly combed hair and bushy mustache. I offered to let him have it but he declined and opted to write down the information on how to get his own copy. He was just one of my many "single serving" friends that I met during my treatments.

CHAPTER 16

"Ofishal"

The goal of fostering is reunification, and in the best-case scenario, foster parents can help mentor not only the children but also the biological parents. As I mentioned in regards to becoming a foster parent, there is at the very least the difficulty of scheduling with the biological parents, and at worst it can include extreme disagreements concerning the well-being of the children. When we began fostering, we didn't anticipate our road ending in adoption as we knew that reunification was always the goal that was sought after. We learned what it meant to pray without ceasing as we prayed for the circumstances to change, for the parents to find healing (physically, mentally, and spiritually) and to become a safe haven for their children; one that we could feel confident in if/when the children returned.

That first year of fostering, the days turned into weeks and weeks turned into months, and months turned into seasons without word or contact from parents, and our prayers began to shift. It was a real wrestle with God as each passing day went by. You never want a person to fail, but we also couldn't *imagine seeing these children we loved so much return home at this point. They had grown so much; they had learned to talk; they had learned to trust; they had learned to smile, laugh, and play freely. Our prayers turned to asking God to do unimaginable good on behalf of them and their family.*

Many children in foster care have inherited a legacy of drug abuse, neglect, and trauma. As foster parents, you feel an urgency to break the cycle and give the kids in your care a step ahead, and to show them and their family what a life lived in the light can look like. That can be so much more difficult than we ever anticipated, Whitney and I both have our struggles and baggage which weigh us down, and distracts us from the goal of being the light bearers and signposts to the way of Jesus that we would want to be. And, then pile on the Cancer diagnosis which only made things more difficult.

All of our meetings with DCS took place about an hour away from our home. So, when there was a meeting on a treatment day, I would have a two-hour treatment 30 minutes south in Huntsville and then travel another hour in the other direction for meetings that never seemed to accomplish what we had hoped and prayed for, "unimaginable good." It was tiresome, and that was just the physical aspect. There is a mental side as well. We just didn't know what the outcome was going to be. To say we were sitting on our hands and being patient would be wrong. We labored in prayer over this situation continually, and what proved to be the most difficult was that no one seemed to be moving as fast as we wanted them to. The nature of foster care is just messy. It's a system built to help people who have hit the bottom. So, you can imagine that nothing in the foster care world is ever perfect because it deals with broken humans in a very broken world. We saw mistakes everywhere (including our own) and it is hard to sit back when it looks like the only people paying for those mistakes were the kids. Trusting the process in this situation was difficult to say the least. One of the hardest parts for me was to keep my eye on the goal. We wanted the kids and their family to know Christ, to feel his love, and be safe.

There were many nights I questioned how we were going to make it with these two young ones. Days when my frustration with them was evident. Nights when my frustrations with the situation due to the choices of others was high, and moments when I'd had enough of the meetings. But God had molded our hearts into a home for these kiddos. We loved and wanted Hailee and Daniel to be Creasys.

The kids had been in our home for 18 months on the day of my diagnosis, three months longer than the federal deadline for filing termination, yet nothing seemed to budge. We knew that a change would have to happen soon, but we had no idea what it would look like. We prayed continually for God to favor them, to work unimaginable good on their behalf, and to preserve the little family in our home.

***

On Wednesday December 12, 2018, while we were walking in Stonebridge Park after one of the kids' speech therapy appointments, we got a phone call that would forever change our lives. We had a particularly awkward meeting the previous week with everyone involved in Hailee and Daniel's case. Travis left that meeting even more hopeless that the kids' situation would ever get resolved, but I felt like the DCS workers had concluded that the children couldn't be left hanging in the balance much longer and that steps toward permanency needed to happen. But I felt like it would require a long court process for the children to finally have permanency, and I knew that would be difficult on everyone involved.

The phone call in Stonebridge Park that day came as a complete shock when we heard Hailee and Daniel's biological mom on the other end of the phone. She said that she had had a lot of time to think about the situation and she felt that God told her to allow us to adopt the kids. She reassured me that she wouldn't change her mind. Their mother felt that the biological father would do the same, and said that she would encourage him to do so. She had already set the date to surrender her rights with the judge.

To say it was sudden is an understatement. We were completely shocked. We had never experienced what seemed like such a sudden answer to prayer. God just parted the waters so we could walk right through it; we didn't have to wade through the waters of a long, ugly court battle, we were able to just walk right through the process on a dry path to the kids' adoption date seven months later. We really saw Exodus 14:14 at work just like we saw it in the hospital, "The Lord will fight for you, you need only to be still."

I had to quit striving and stewing and obsessing over the situation in the hospital because I could no longer carry the emotional burden of it. It made me finally just give it up in prayer to God and trust that He would take care of the kids in the best way, and on December 12, 2018, I knew that He had done a miracle through speaking to their mother's heart and giving her the courage to make such a selfless and sacrificial decision.

When we got in the car that afternoon, Lauren Daigle's song, "O, Lord" was playing on the local KLove radio station, the same song I had sung to myself and over the kids' situation when everything seemed to be going wrong and we seemed to be surrounded by darkness. It felt like a wink from God, like He was saying, "Hey remember when you sang all those words. 'I will stand my ground where hope can be found. You'll take all that is wrong and make it right. Your strength is found at the end of my road. Your grace, it reaches to the hurting. Still through the tears and the questioning why, I will stand my ground where hope can be found.'[1] I heard those prayers and I've been listening and working the whole time even when you felt like I wasn't.'" Not coincidentally, the same song played on the radio when we got in the car after leaving our lawyer's office to sign the papers that set up our adoption date six months later.

***

Prior to fostering our kiddos, I celebrated just about every minor event. Prior to my Leukemia diagnosis we would celebrate events at our house. Now we REALLY celebrate every little event! Our celebrations vary from a full-blown party with blow-up water slide to just enjoying the occasional Dr. Pepper or Vanilla Coke for the small victories. As a person who loves to celebrate, I'm fascinated by the celebrations of the Bible. From David's full blown five-alarm-fire circus party during the return of the Ark of the Covenant (2 Samuel 6:14-22) to the rejoicing of the angels when one sinner repents (Luke 15:10), the response is amazing. Maybe it's my "enneagram seven" bias but I think we undersell the excitement we should show in this life. It really is a win-win that Paul describes in his "to live is Christ and to die is gain" statement (Philippians 1:18-21). I'm not saying we shouldn't mourn when the time is right (2 Samuel 6:1-12) but Paul sitting in a jail cell exhorts or as some would put it, directly commands us to rejoice multiple times (Philippians 4:4). Times were tough and it was hard to ignore that. Life is hard but God has equipped us with his Spirit, the Spirit of power (2 Timothy 1:7)! It's the same Spirit that caused John the Baptist to leap within his mother's womb as Mary approached with Jesus in her belly (Luke 1:41). It's the same Spirit that was on David when the Ark approached and the same Spirit that raised Jesus from the dead (Romans 8:11). That same Spirit indwells you as a Christian and makes you the Temple of God (1 Corinthians 6:19-20). Once again, our time to celebrate a day we thought might not ever come, came on July 2, 2019. Adoption day.

***

My personality is different from Travis'. He has had to teach me to stop and celebrate. I have typically lived my life with various goals, and once I reached them I took a deep breath, and then began looking around to figure out what I need to work on next. Honestly, I think that part of my personality drives him crazy, but he has shown me the beauty in stopping to properly celebrate. In fact, I've recently begun to think of celebration as a spiritual discipline especially when it relates to answered prayer. Celebration and thanksgiving to God for his blessing and favor glorifies him.

So, on July 2, 2019, we threw a big party to celebrate

God's kindness to our family. Just a few months earlier I had feared that I could possibly be left alone, but on July 2, 2019, God legally made us a family. The kids still refer to their adoption party as their "Creasy Party." They were only three- and four-years-old at the time, so the main thing they understood was that their names would now match ours.

The party had a fish theme since the kids were "Ofishally Ours." We set up tables under the large shade trees in our front yard for all our friends and family to mix and mingle and enjoy their food and conversation. My grandparents rented a blowup water slide for the backyard, and the RCA football players helped us set it up and test it out the night before the party. We decorated with large mermaid and narwhal balloons, a fishing net with pictures of the children clothes pinned to it, a balloon arch made from balloons of all different shades of blue, and a long banner that read, "It's O-fish-al, Hailee Elizabeth Renee Creasy and Daniel Wade Creasy."

Our friends and family were all invited to attend the adoption ceremony at the Lincoln County Courthouse and then join us for the brunch party at our house afterward. Everyone arrived at the Courthouse early. The basement courtroom was packed beyond capacity with people who had prayed for this day to come for years.

Everyone wore matching t-shirts for the occasion that said, "We are the village" because they had all been the village that helped us raise Hailee and Daniel since they came to our home more than two years earlier. I remember Hailee asking, "Are we Creasy's now?" At the end of the ceremony and Judge Cox answering, "Yes! You are!" We took our first official family picture with Judge Cox and our lawyer, Mr.

Simms, with a letter board sign that read, "Today, our names match! July 2, 2019 #TeamCreasy."

When the formalities were complete and we made our way back home to the party with our friends and family, I felt a lightness that I had forgotten about. A weight was removed from my shoulders that I didn't really know I had been carrying around. Our kids were now legally our family.

Back at our house, as the party got started everyone gathered in our living room for a prayer before eating. As we stood there thanking God for this good and perfect gift, I remembered standing in that very same room the day we purchased our house and moved in. Travis offered a prayer before we began moving in all our belongings and setting about making the new-to-us 1970s split-level house our home. In the prayer he prayed that our home would be a blessing to many. As I looked around at all the friends and family who were gathered there, I realized that this home had not only been a blessing to the two traumatized little babies who had shown up on the doorstep near midnight on Easter Sunday two years earlier, it was a blessing to all of those who had interceded for us in prayer. Here they were seeing the fruit of their prayers and celebrating God's kindness in what had seemed like an impossible situation just a few months prior.

I think of that little "O-Fish-Al Party" as an Ebenezer of sorts for myself and a lot of my loved ones. The word Ebenezer is a Hebrew word that means "Stone of Help." It is used in 1 Samuel 7 when Samuel sets up a stone to commemorate the help God gave the Israelites in a miraculous defeat of the Philistines (1 Samuel 7:12). Our loved ones took pictures with a chalk board on which they wrote messages about what the day meant to them. My siblings' sign said, "Today, we saw faith become sight." My great aunt and uncle's sign said, "Today, we know the reward is worth the risk," and the one that makes my eyes well with tears and knot come up in my throat every time was my mother's sign, "Today, I know why 4/17/17 felt like I met my grandkids. I did."

ENDNOTES

[1] Daigle, Lauren. "Oh Lord." Track #2 How Can It Be. Centricity Music, 2015, Compact Disc.

CHAPTER 17

Finish

As long as I can remember I've attended the church
of Christ. Some of my earliest memories come from
attending New Hope Church of Christ in Florence,
Alabama. During my preteen years, we moved our member-
ship to Jacksonburg Church of Christ where I joined youth
group with my good friend Ben. It was a small, tight knit
group that just enjoyed hanging out with one another. We sat
on the front row during services and the young men would
lead songs at the beginning of Sunday night services.

I started attending Maywood Christian Camp in Hamil-
ton, Alabama. One tradition at camp was for Seniors during
the last night of the week's bonfire to stand up and talk about
their experience at camp. Following the tradition, I got up and
shared. I believe it was Ben who went back and informed our
pulpit minister Gary Gooch that I had addressed the camp.

Gary persistently asked me to preach my first sermon.
Gary had called me out of the crowd to assist in VBS songs at
various times so I finally relented, and I agreed to attempt a
sermon. I bombed horribly. Until that point, I don't believe I

had ever been that nervous. I got up and basically said, "The Bible says that drinking and tattoos are wrong" repeatedly for ten minutes. I sat down doing my best to hold back the tears as my youth minister Doug Jackson bragged about my bravery. I could no longer hold them back. And that is where I thought my future in ministry died.

God had another plan. Twenty-two years later, I'm still preaching and teaching. When Ben and I became too old to attend Maywood as campers, we became counselors. Someone in charge at our week of camp thought, "Surely, those guys have no ego and they would make complete fools of themselves for a good laugh. What could possibly go wrong by giving them the stage in front of impressionable preteens and teenagers?"

Apparently, we didn't mess it up too bad because eventually Larry Davenport convinced the Challenge Youth Conference board to give us microphones to perfect our goofiness in front of over ten thousand people from all over the United States. Challenge Youth Conference also known as "CYC" is a weekend-long conference for Church of Christ teenagers in the Smokey Mountains of Tennessee during February each year. CYC has branched out to Dallas, Texas over the last few years. I have brothers and sisters all over the world because his Kingdom knows no boundaries.

During my hospital stay it seemed like every one of those brothers and sisters were writing me cards. I knew a great number of them were praying for my well-being. At times that "great cloud of witnesses" was so vivid I could see them and certainly feel them. It wasn't long before a "CYC Loves Travis" shirt design was out on the market. I was praying for an opportunity to express my love for them as well.

The hospital mail ladies felt the burden of prayers too. On more than one occasion they asked if I was a rockstar or celebrity because of the amount of mail they delivered to my room. It was a highlight each day to dig through those envelopes of well-wishers and friends; there were some heartfelt messages that moved me deeply. Why would this stranger or that stranger take time out of their busy lives and write such a powerful encouraging message? Other messages were absolutely hilarious. Some had impactful scriptures that would soon adorn my walls. I read them all.

Stunningly, there was no hate mail that I can remember. Honestly a little disappointing considering just a few years ago I sang my special edition of "Rocky Top" entitled "Rocky Flop" at CYC less than an hour from Knoxville. The chorus goes, "Rocky flop you'll always be, the worst in the SEC." The boos and jeers rained down all around me; it was wonderful. Just a few months later, dressed in my American flag designed suit including sport coat, pants, and matching tie, purchased by the RCA class of 2023, I would get a standing ovation from some of the same people that encouraged me. It's refreshing when you run into people who can take a joke.

It's overwhelming when you have people willingly in your life who love you despite all the evidence to why they shouldn't. I'm thankful for those cards and all the emotions that came through my door along with them. It was a wonderful reminder that the world wasn't completely passing me by. Another daily activity included listening to the "My Mother's Hymn Book" album by Johnny Cash. Especially his rendition of "Let the Lower Lights Be Burning." I embodied the "some poor fainting struggling seaman"[1] during this season of my life. Those folks who took time to pray, visit, call or write were the lower lights that saw me through. You may not think those actions matter but they do.

In fact, I get very angry when I see people poke fun or disregard the phrase "thoughts and prayers" on social media. Sure, there are some people who just say those things because they don't know what else to say. Some have no intention of following through but that doesn't negate the power of prayer.

In Hebrews 12:1, it speaks about a great cloud of witnesses that encourage us as we go throughout our journey. Some of those in the crowd are the people mentioned in the Bible, some are the unnamed throng that have gone on before us. Others are like those mentioned in the previous paragraphs. Those we have an intimate relationship with and know how to push us onward. In the second verse of the chapter, it tells us that Jesus is the "author and finisher of our faith" who we turn to when it is time to move upward. He taught us how to finish even when it is difficult.

Just because something is difficult, doesn't mean you should shut the door on it. Football was my first love. Some of my earliest memories are watching whatever football game was on my television. You read that right, "game" as in there was typically only one televised game on at a time. This was before ESPN the Ocho. Let's just say that the Crimson Tide was not always on my television. My Saturday morning routine involved cereal, Saturday morning cartoons, WWE (back then it was the Federation), the Alabama/Auburn athletics shows and then the Jefferson Pilot game of the week. If that game didn't feature Alabama, I was outside mimicking the plays called by Eli Gold through the radio in whatever vehicle was parked out front. Spin moves, jukes and hurdles were all a part of my skill set as I "played" for Alabama every

Saturday. Siran Stacy was my favorite player as a kid until David Palmer showed up wearing that beautiful #2 on his chest and winning a national championship in 1992. I just knew that I'd play at Bryant-Denny Stadium (Alabama played their home games there when they were not at Legion Field). Preferably with my best friend, first cousin and QB Ben Hayes. The only real question was who would get to wear the #2 at the Capstone?

When you don't break 100 pounds until you are a Senior in High School those dreams fade pretty quickly. Throw in the fact that at the time Mars Hill Bible School where Ben attended didn't even have a football team. That didn't stop us from playing backyard tackle football every chance we got. In fact, I knocked myself out at one of my preteen birthday parties because I broke a strict rule of football. I had possession of the ball and was approaching the goal line aka our front porch, and I committed a football sin by looking back to see who the nearest defender was. As I turned back around, I ran into a column on my front porch and collapsed to the ground—out cold. Reminder to Lot's wife, Travis, and future football players, don't look back!

Once Bill Walsh's College Football became available on Sega Genesis a whole new world opened up. You had the option to play as any national champion or great team from the past. If my memory is accurate, the only mode was exhibition mode where one player could play against the computer or another player. Ben and I quickly turned this into our first "coaching job." Of course, we were the Offensive and Defensive Coordinators of the 1992 National Champions. We would organize the seasons, the top 25 and the postseason. Ben would call me on our house phone, he would call the offense and I would coor-

dinate that stellar defense! Did we create the first "online" dynasty mode? We should've claimed it.

Despite having the body of a horse jockey, along with the help of the movie "Little Giants," Ben convinced me that I should play football as a freshman at Central High School. My mom agreed to let me go through Spring practice, certain that they'd never let me play because of my size. To her surprise and my happiness, they didn't make cuts in football. You survive and you get a spot on the team. I quickly began to realize what they meant when they said "survive." As a freshman I was on the Junior Varsity team which won two games. Our coach told us that he was just getting us ready for Varsity, so we basically conditioned for half of practice. I was introduced to the term "gasser." That word that can only be uttered with glee by coaches or "the dread of the LORD " and a sneer by players. I've lived long enough to experience both. "Gassers" could make Voldemort weep and want his momma.

Gassers were sprints from one sideline of the football field to the other, back, over, and back again. That's 53 1/3 yards one way so 213 yards total. We ran so much we had kids dropping out left and right. Most players who tried to quit were successful because the coaches didn't make much effort to keep them. One day, one of our bigger players on that JV team had finally had his fill. He just laid down at the starting line. He was a very important member of our team who the coach didn't feel like we could afford to lose. More like the varsity coach had made it clear that he was one of the ones who better survive. The JV coach began barking orders for one of his teammates to get him "through" the drill. Wouldn't you know it, the nearest teammate was a 60-pound Travis Creasy. Did I mention the kid at the very least doubled my weight? There I *was with this guy's forearm draped over my shoulder pads, desperately trying to get traction enough to drag this dude. I actually got him through 3/4 of the trip over before he finally pulled his weight.*

As you would imagine, I didn't play very much. Now that I've been a coach, it was probably in my best interest to not see the field very much—they didn't want my blood on their hands. I practiced as a wide receiver and defensive back for most of my career. Wide receivers catch the ball out towards the sideline/numbers on a football field and they also block out there as well. As our team was mainly a running team; there was a lot of blocking to do. Defensive backs defend against the pass, so they try to keep the wide receivers from catching the ball.

I was content with my role on the team until one day my defensive back coach told me I was wasting my time which really meant I was wasting his time. He had played in a Super Bowl for Washington if my memory serves me correctly. Who was going to argue with that?

I was crushed. I wanted to quit. I went home upset and crying. Mom really didn't know what to do so she had my dad come over and try to talk me out of quitting. I don't remember what he said, but I ended up sticking with it. A few years later I learned that mom had asked Ben's dad to go and speak to the Head Coach. Thank God I didn't know, I would never have shown my face again. I decided that since I was going to focus mainly on playing wide receiver that I would do every-thing in my power to make that coach regret his decision. Unfortunately for his defensive backs (who were also my friends) that meant taking out my frustrations on them. I can promise it wasn't anything too nefarious but plenty annoying.

I did not see a lot of playing time as an underclassman, but I still got what I was looking for in being a part of a team. I had plenty of coaches who looked out for me but also pushed me to be the best I could be. I was truly introduced to outlaw country tunes of Coe, Waylon, Willie and Cash as sung by my teammates during warm-ups. The band "Alabama" was sung loudly following road victories. Those songs transport me back to those humid "dog days of Summer" filled with two-a-day practices. Those days were rough, stinky and painful at times, but they would influence me to always finish what I start.

It is those seasons that make me less than compassionate for players who complain about playing time. In sports, "waiting your turn" is almost a memory of the past. I would say that "waiting" does not encompass how hard you are working to get your opportunity to play. In my football career "waiting" involved conditioning, lifting weights, and doing all the things the starters did but with little playing time. As an adult it might be doing all the right things and not being able to have children or being the best spouse you can be and getting nothing in return. As in life, it is often the most diffi-cult to delay gratification, but football taught me that anything worth doing is going to be difficult. If you do every-thing to finish what you start, you are already one step ahead of the competition.

My senior year rolled around, and I finally broke the century mark on the scales. I might have surpassed 5 feet in height. My last shot would be my best shot. I was going to take as many opportunities as I could get. Either way I was not going to waste one second of playing time. I wore the number 12 on that JV squad, but I traded it in for the number 83 upon joining the high school team my sophomore year. I believe

I had the number that Ben Hayes' dad wore when he played for the same school.

For 3 years I had been the biggest "smallest and pom-pom-less" cheerleader at the games. It was now time for this Central High School "save the best for last" class of 1999 senior to take his place among the immortals of football fame. There I was on the cover of the program with my classmates and Head Coach, Ikey Fowler. The black and white photo filtered the red home jersey with the no outline, block "83" number on the front and sleeves, the white pants and red knee-high socks. My red helmet with black facemask sits in my classroom as a good reminder of the tenacity of that little guy.

I was able to work my way into the rotation at wide receiver, or my coaches just felt sorry for me. The other wide receivers and I would take turns running out to the huddle to inform the quarterback of the play to run. We would line up and run the play then get replaced by the next wide receiver with the next play. We were mainly a running team, so I had to be good at blocking to gain more playing time. If we ever threw the ball, I typically wasn't in the game as we had more athletic guys to catch the ball.

The only pass thrown to me as an underclassman occurred during a spring scrimmage with another high school. I caught it and scored a touchdown. To let you know how odd this was, my mom didn't believe my grandmother when she informed her of my small victory. It was the only action of my football career my mom missed.

I was three or four weeks into my final shot when I fractured my wrist during practice. I can't even tell you it was a brutal hit, though I would love to. However, I was running across the field to catch a pass which was under thrown and as

I tried to break my stride, somehow I ended up falling backwards and instead of allowing my tailbone pad do what it was created to do, I tried to catch myself. As I sat in the coach's office while the rest of my teammates practiced, I desperately tried to get my wrist to function under that ice pack. The more I moved it the more my stomach sank.

Eventually I was able to get into the Bone and Joint Clinic and the doctor broke the terrible news that my playing days were effectively over. After I punched him in the face repeatedly in my mind, I started to cry. They came in and stuck a needle in my wrist that looked like it would poke through the other side to numb my pain. It failed to numb the pain at the core of my being. Before they had set my wrist and slapped a bulky cast on it, I had already made up my mind that I was going to do everything in my arsenal to play again. Unfortunately lying was not off the table. I'm repenting right now, Coach.

I was able to convince everyone that I'd be back in two to three weeks. I think the fact I wasn't that big of a contributor probably helped in my deception. Sure enough, I was back in a couple of weeks, just in time to play Deshler. I remember my excitement was somewhat dashed when it looked like the Alabama Crimson Tide was coming down the hill from the Deshler locker room instead of a group of high school kids. My fire was rekindled as I got to be a captain. One of Deshler's captains kind of laughed when he saw my clunky super softened cast. I memorized his number and waited for my opportunity at revenge.

I didn't play in the first half, and I wasn't alone. No one played up to their potential and we were getting beaten pretty badly by halftime. Coach Fowler threw me a bone at halftime when he told me to get ready to play. All I could think was I can't wait to get my shot at that guy who laughed at me. The first play I got him and one of his buddies with brutal blocks. Being short and off the radar had its benefits as I was able to give them both "legal hits" by 1990's standards, plus, I was more than a little vindictive in those days. I believe that loss effectively ended our playoff hopes. We would eventually finish 6-4 in our first season as our school moved up to a higher division with larger schools.

We rolled into our last game with pride on the line. We played Sheffield in our home stadium for my last high school game. It was a close game in the second half, and I had been filling my normal role and trying to soak it all up. I noticed when I was on the field, they didn't assign a defensive back to defend me on offense. Not sure if this was a coaching decision or the guy who was assigned to me didn't think I was worth his time. Whatever it was, it didn't sit well with me. I went to the offensive coordinator, Coach Mayfield, and pointed it out to him a few times. If I remember correctly, one of my teammates confirmed my account of what was going on. The next thing he said was a blur because it had to sink in that he just said, "Tell Hamm to throw it to Creasy."

I vaguely remember looking up to the crowd and thinking this is going to blow my mom's mind. I snapped back to reality when the thought of "now you have to catch it" crossed my scattered mind. I told our quarterback Jeff Hamm exactly what the coach had said. As the huddle broke and I made my way over to line up between the field numbers and our sideline I began to hope that I didn't misunderstand Coach Mayfield. It was too late by then anyway. The ball snapped and just like in the movies everything was in slow motion. Slower than my usual slow-foot speed. I ran to my spot and turned to catch the ball with one hand and a bulky club-shaped cast. One of my lasting memories is watching the white stripe on the football spinning in a perfect spiral. "Is it ever going to get here?" "Is it going to get here before the defender does?" THUD! The ball stuck in my chest and I "alligator armed" that wonderful pass as the defender arrived and stopped me one yard short of the goal line. After the ringing in my ears and shock cleared, I could distinctly hear my mom screaming. We scored on the next play and never trailed again. I used to think about how awesome it would've been to score had I not had that cast and could've stretched the ball across the goal line. Now I understand that without the cast resulting in the defender's lack of attention to me I might never have been thrown the pass.

During the last practice week of my high school career, Coach Fowler talked about visualizing ourselves making the play. Not sure what prompted him to talk so much about it that week. Maybe he had talked about it before, but my high school brain just didn't hear it, but I tried it out the night before that Sheffield game. To say the least I've believed in that approach ever since. That Thursday night, it was visualizing catching a pass. On a random day in October years later, it would be visualizing the ringing of a bell.

Winning is a wonderful feeling. I've experienced it and it is addictive. As a young man I had a desire to be a part of a team. Things haven't changed much, but the definition of "winning" has changed as I get older. There are individual wins and team wins. You get enough individual wins, and they typically result in team wins. I want the team to win and will sacrifice to make it happen. Sacrifice often involves delivering bad news or at least truths no one wants to hear. As a coach, it was on me to be honest with my players. As an oncologist, I can't imagine how much bad news Dr. Diaz delivers in a 24-hour period. On October 16, 2018, my definition of "winning," "finishing" and "hard truth" changed forever. Winning a JV Football game that night quickly became an afterthought. I still don't know the outcome of that particular game. Football fell a little further down my priority list. Football might not be the priority it once was, but the lessons learned have stuck with me.

Fast forward 5 months and I would get my turn to ring the bell (unless of course someone else did what I had wanted to do and rang it off the wall). 80 plus treatments later and I got the same satisfaction with the same amount of fanfare if not a little more since I had family and friends join. We ate buffalo wings, and I had a Dr. Pepper and enjoyed some Reese's Cups (a treatment friend brought me a pound of Reese's cups).

In that journey the writer of the biblical statement, "Better is the end of a thing than its beginning, and the patient in spirit is better than the proud in spirit" certainly rang true! (Ecclesiastes 7:8). My Cancer journey may never truly be over as I continue to process the events and check off more milestones. Some days it's like that "Cancer Guy" never existed and some days I'm hit with "scanxiety" out of nowhere.

The words that Jesus said, "But the one who endures to the end will be saved" mean more and more every day (Matthew 24:13). Life can be difficult, but Jesus does simplify a lot of things when he makes statements like the previous. Notice I said "simplify." Simple doesn't always equate to easy. One of the events that the wise man and foolish man had in common was that the storms came (Matthew 7:24-27). The difference was their foundation and who they "hung onto for dear life" when the storms raged.

The Apostle Paul had experience with storms. He was able to write to his dear friend Timothy, "I have fought the good fight, I have finished the race, I have kept the faith" (2 Timothy 4:7). His storms were actual weather events (Acts 27:18), bodily pain and spiritual/emotional trials (Acts 16:37).

As I write this, I'm overwhelmed with the thought of the worldwide struggles that are faced daily. My encouragement to you is to hang on to whatever gets you through it. My hope is that you are holding onto the only person that has overcome death, returned to encourage those he left behind and will return triumphantly once again (Hebrews 12:2).

ENDNOTES

[1] Cash, Johnny. "Let the Lower Lights Be Burning." Track #9 My Mother's Hymn Book. Universal Music Publishing Group, Warner Chappell Music, Inc, 2004, Compact Disc.

CHAPTER 18

Trust & Obey

O bedience is just tough. I remember when I was in elementary school, my parents got my sister and I a beautiful chocolate lab puppy. Well, Santa Claus got us a chocolate Labrador retriever puppy. My mom recently digitized all of our 8-millimeter tape home videos, so the scene is fresh in my memory. The bottom right corner of the screen says it is December 25, 1992. My sister and I were happily playing with the toys Santa had brought us, and my dad walked down the stairs and into the living room. He went straight over to a table next to the fireplace where Santa's empty milk mug and cookie plate were sitting and picked up a hand-written note from the big man himself! The note said there was one more surprise in the garage. We all made a beeline for the garage and came back inside with the most beautiful, floppy-eared, big-pawed, chocolate lab puppy. My sister Bailey can be heard joyously shouting that we should name him chocolate cake (she was obsessed with Little Debbie Swiss Cake Rolls at the time), to which my dad answers that Santa said his name was Willy. I would later learn that my dad had actually named him after one of his buddies from high school football.

Willy grew quickly, and by the Spring he was already much bigger than me. He was a loving and loyal dog, but he was extremely energetic and had a bad habit of wandering. My mom enrolled him in an obedience class at Snead State, the local community college, to help train him to respond to commands. They went to class once per week and worked diligently on his homework every afternoon. He learned the basics of sit, lie down, stay, and how to walk on a leash. The obedience classes were great, but I remember hating the choke collar. Just the sight of it made me sad. Willy was a large muscular dog, by the time he was full grown he weighed nearly 100 pounds, so his choke collar was rather large and looked like a medieval torture device. It was made of metal prongs that "hinged" together, and every time Willy pulled on his leash the prongs would tighten around his neck. I did not enjoy watching mom and Willy practice leash walking because he was so energetic and bouncy that every-thing seemed to catch his attention and off he would go in the direction of the squirrel, stray cat, or butterfly that made its way across his path, and the collar would tighten down around his neck every time. I would always think, "Willy, just stay next to mom without trying to get ahead. Every time you try to run off without her or disobey her commands you get hurt!"

I used to have this idea that as long as I was being obedient to God and his call on my life that my life would go smoothly. I didn't necessarily believe that bad things would never happen, but I did believe that if I was doing God's will that whatever mission He had called me to would just come naturally. I can't tell you how many times I've heard people talk about God "closing doors," meaning they tried something they felt God had called them to and it just didn't work out on the first go, or it was a lot more difficult than they had imagined.

This theology made a lot of sense to me until I started really studying the Bible. A life of obedience to God didn't mean an easy street for Joseph. Joseph was faithful to God amid extreme temptation. His boss's wife continually tried to seduce him, and one day when she had finally reached her wit's end and reached out to grab him, he ran away leaving his clothes in her hands. You know what Joseph was most concerned with? I would think that he would be concerned with losing his job or possibly even his life if his boss found out, but his character and love for God was stronger than that. As he runs away from the temptation, Joseph says, "How could I sin against God in this way?" Sadly, the humiliated woman framed Joseph and said he tried to take advantage of her and then Joseph ended up in a prison cell. But the Bible tells us, "The Lord was with Joseph and showed him steadfast love and gave him favor in the sight of the keeper of the prison" (Genesis 39:21).

How about Elijah? Elijah was obedient to God's call to challenge the prophets of Baal to a showdown on Mt. Carmel. The scene is like a Western of epic proportions. Evil King Ahab and his wife Jezebel call together 450 prophets of Baal and Elijah threw down his challenge. He asked the people of Israel, "How long will you go limping between two different opinions? If the Lord is God, follow him; but if Baal, then follow him." Elijah then challenged the prophets of Baal to a contest: they would call to their god, and he would call to *the* God, and whoever answered by fire and burned up the sacrifice on the altar was the one true God. All the people agreed, and the spectacle began. Baal's prophets got to go first. They put on a good show; calling out to Baal, limping around the altar, cutting themselves with swords until the blood flowed, and raving on for hours. Elijah then took over, and rather than go for a simple win he doused the whole altar in water three times before he prayed. When he prayed, God answered mightily; He not only burned up the sacrifice, but also the wood, the stones, and the dust and licked up the water in the trench. All the people fell on their faces and proclaimed, "The Lord, He is God."

Sounds like a win for Elijah to me! But do you know what Elijah did next? He literally ran for his life because Jezebel threatened to kill him by the same time the next day. The man who just watched God defeat 450 prophets of Baal was afraid that God wouldn't protect him from a single woman. Elijah ran, sat down under a broom tree, and then prayed to God that he would just die. God actually never answered that prayer with a yes. Elijah never died; he was taken up by a whirlwind into heaven. Instead, God answered Elijah's prayer with an angel who was sent to minister to him, and who brought him into God's presence at Mt. Horeb where the Lord spoke to him in a still small voice (1 Kings 18-19).

How about a New Testament example? Jesus's beloved disciple, John was obedient to death. We know Jesus must have trusted John because he left his mother, Mary, in John's care when he was on the cross (John 19:25-27). We know from early church history that John was a faithful teacher and elder for many years in the church at Ephesus. We also know that he was exiled to the island of Patmos in his old age because of his obedience to Christ (Revelation 1:9). While on the island John is visited by Jesus in a vision. Jesus relays the message of victory that is the book of Revelation for John to write down and send to the seven churches of Asia for their encouragement (Revelation 1:9-11).

Joseph, Elijah, and John were all obedient. They were all in the center of God's will for their lives, but their obedience came with hardship in the form of imprisonment, a death threat, and exile. Did you notice there was one other constant in their three stories? God was present with each of them in their hardship. God showed Joseph steadfast love and gave him favor in the sight of the prison keeper (Genesis 39:21). God ministered to Elijah through an angel and then revealed his presence in a still, small voice on Mt. Horeb (1 Kings 19:7-18). Jesus appeared to John on the island of Patmos with a message of encouragement for His church (Revelation). So, they all faced hardship in their obedience, but they didn't have to go at it alone.

We learned obedience to God's call is usually tougher than you expect during our foster care journey. When we both got on board and said yes to God's invitation to join him in the work of fostering; we didn't know how difficult that "yes" would be.

I remember leaving my house to go for a run one humid summer morning soon after Hailee and Daniel came to live with us. It was one of those mornings when you only need to step outside for a minute or two before you start to feel wet from the heat and humidity. I thought about going back inside and calling it quits on my run because the weather was miserable, but I had some things I needed to have a talk with God about and pounding the asphalt in the quiet on my rural Tennessee road was the place I felt most at-home with God, the place where the words that really truly go through my brain would actually come out of my mouth. I've always wondered what people think when they pass me on the road. It is not uncommon for me to be deep in conversation with God as I run. Hopefully, people just assume I am singing along with some music rather than thinking I am a crazy person. That particular day I asked God if I had gotten the fostering thing all wrong. I asked if I had misunderstood because surely, I wasn't the best he could do for the job. I told God I felt like this was a longer-term commitment than we had originally thought, and that I was on the struggle bus. I told him he had to do some work on my heart if this was his plan because I just felt like I wasn't cut out for what he had called me to.

Foster parenting got easier logistically as we got into a groove with a schedule, and we began to understand the kids and communicate with them better and the kids grew to trust us and their new community. But, as the logistics got easier, the emotional part got tougher. As we fell more and more in love with our two kiddos, the tougher it got to think about them going back to their biological parents. The difficulties were different, and spiritually challenging.

Then, at the height of the emotional turmoil I felt over losing the kids, Travis was diagnosed with cancer. There were a couple of times I felt like it was all a really terrible dream that I would eventually wake up from. It seemed unfair. At first glance, it seemed like our "yes" to foster parenting had been met with suffering. Deep down, I knew that wasn't the case, but it did not keep me from having moments of anger with God over the circumstance.

But, wow, God was present with us during this time. Like Joseph, we felt God's favor in so many ways. Dr. Diaz and Cleo, his nurse practitioner, may be as personal, kind, and cautious with every patient as they were with Travis, but I felt like we had favor with them. I can only attribute that to God. One day, Travis' nurse told us that she had to fight off another nurse to get to take care of him for the day, God's favor. DCS went above and beyond to help us keep the children in our home by performing timely background checks on our relatives and friends who offered to take care of the children, God's favor. Our coworkers at RCA donated personal days and sick leave to Travis to keep him from missing a paycheck, God's favor.

God provided for our physical needs above and beyond what we could ask or imagine, and we heard his voice through scripture that seemed to speak directly to our hearts, just like He provided for Elijah through an angel in his season of exhaustion and spoke to him in a still, small voice. God provided for our financial needs through many generous people. Thanks to so many organizations, friends and family members, we made it through Travis' leukemia diagnosis and treatment with no medical debt. Many people volunteered to help us in our fostering journey by giving us items that were needed for our home study process and babysitting the kids when we had no daycare options. During the early days of our foster care journey and after Travis' return home from the hospital many people offered to help us with meals as we got acclimated to our new normal. God spoke directly to our hearts through many different scriptures during these seasons. The Holy Spirit would make certain scriptures seem to jump off the page. It was as if when we read, the Holy Spirit grabbed our attention and said, listen up, this one's for you. The day I went to tour Kingdom Kids Learning Center, the daycare where our babies would eventually attend, I sat in my car in the parking lot waiting for my appointment time. I had spoken with Rasheta, the director of the daycare the day before. She had told me I could come in at 8:00 the next morning. I was a little early for my appointment because I wasn't exactly sure how long it would take me to get there. I was beyond exhausted. Daniel wasn't sleeping well at night, and my mind was frazzled from the constant needs of two babies during the daytime hours. I told God I needed a word of encouragement from him, and I opened the Bible app on my phone, closed my eyes, and put my finger on the list of books of the Bible to randomly choose one. My finger landed on Matthew. When I clicked on Matthew, the app showed me the 28 chapters in the book, so I closed my eyes again, circled my finger around and tapped on the chapter my finger landed on, chapter 18. I began reading in the first verse, but I got a little chill and the hair stood up on my arm when I read this, "Whoever receives and welcomes one child like this in My name receives Me" (Matthew 18:5, NKJV). In the fall of 2018, God spoke to me through the repetition of Romans 12:12. In the weeks leading up to Travis' diagnosis the words, "Rejoice in hope, be patient in tribulation, be constant in prayer" were everywhere I turned. I knew the words were important for me, but I didn't quite understand just how crucial they would be to our ability to thrive through the long days in the hospital and in treatment while

Travis was sick. And finally, "The Lord will fight for you, you have only to be still." (Exodus 14:14, NIV) became a promise that we circled as I said earlier. We knew God was working, and that it was time for us to rest in our faith and trust in him.

We also felt God's presence through the prayers and encouragement that poured in from our brothers and sisters in Christ, just as I'm sure the Christians suffering in the first century were encouraged by John's Revelation of the victorious Jesus. Travis received so many cards and letters in the mail at the hospital that, as he mentioned, the volunteers who delivered the mail thought he was a celebrity. Each of those messages gave him the drive to keep fighting. Visitors came to keep us company in the hospital every day, and their presence provided encouragement in the form of laughter about things like the good 'ole days of RCA football when we played the defending state champions with 13 players because the swine flu had ravaged the team's roster to serious heartfelt conversations about the goodness of God.

Sometimes, I wish the simplicity of my early understanding of obedience as it related to Willy and my mom in his obedience training were true, but the facts are we can be perfectly obedient to God, staying near to his side without getting distracted by the world and things will still happen that cause suffering. During those times, it's easy for me to get angry with God and feel like he forgot about me like a piece of mail that falls between the car seats or a sock that gets stuck in the couch cushions. But God has been so faithful to show me that He hasn't forgotten me, that he is always with me, and that his promises will not fail. One of God's promises that comes from Travis' favorite chapter of the Bible, Romans 8 is, "I am sure that neither death nor life, nor angels nor rulers nor things present nor things to come nor powers nor height nor depth, nor anything else in all creation, will be able to separate us from the love of God in Christ Jesus our Lord" (Romans 8:38-39). As Paul says here, the hard times *will* come, but God will always be present; the suffering cannot and will not separate us from him.

CHAPTER 19

Constant in Prayer

S peaking of Travis' favorite chapter, another of God's promises from Romans 8 stands out in my mind as a promise that we saw come to life during this season of our journey. This promise is definitely a "coffee mug verse." If you ask a group of people what their favorite Bible verse is, Romans 8:28 will inevitably be someone's answer, "And we know that for those who love God all things work together for good, for those who are called according to his purpose."

A couple of verses earlier in Romans 8:26, Paul writes about how the Holy Spirit helps us in our weakness when we do not know what to pray. I have felt that many times before, especially when Travis was in the hospital. All I could pray was, "God, please help us." I didn't even really know what I needed to feel peace, what was best for the kids, or how I could help Travis, so I didn't know what to pray for. I think Paul gives us a glimpse into the unseen realm in these verses. He is telling us that it's ok when life throws us a curveball and we don't even have the words to pray, because the Holy Spirit has our back and is advocating before God for us even though we don't know which way is up or down. I don't know about you, but that is very comforting to me. Then, Paul tells us in verse 28 that God is taking those prayers and he is orchestrating everything to work together for the good of those who are called according to his purpose.

We saw that repeatedly throughout our journey. I didn't know what to pray for our children. I didn't know what was best for their future, so I offered many prayers asking God to do immeasurable good on their behalf. He did that very thing, but there were many points along the road where the circumstances looked like the opposite was happening, especially when we thought we would have to give them up to another foster home because of Travis' diagnosis and long hospital stay. But God was moving behind the scenes, working out each of the details.

God gives us another glimpse into the realm of the unseen and his working things together for our good in Daniel 10. Daniel is given a word from the Lord about a great conflict, and he begins to mourn and fast for three weeks. Then 21 days later, a man appeared to Daniel. The man told Daniel not to fear that he had been sent to help him understand the word from God, but that he had been held up by the Prince of Persia and Michael the archangel came to help him.

Whoa! Talk about God orchestrating events behind the scenes. I'm sure those three weeks felt long to Daniel. Twenty-one days is a long time to fast and mourn and be confused and possibly worried about something. But this man who appears to Daniel in the story, tells him that he was sent as soon as Daniel started praying, but he got held up along the way, and God dispatched Michael, the archangel to help him make sure that Daniel's prayer was answered and his confusion was relieved.

Rabbit trail, but here we go anyway... I think we sometimes just jump over timelines in the Bible. We read things like Jonah sat in the belly of the great fish for three days and then it spat him out on the beach, and he went on to Nineveh like he was supposed to do in the first place like it is no big deal, but Jonah sat inside a fish's guts for *three days!* What was that like? Did he feel like he would ever see the light of day again? Did he know that he would not die in there? Did he have a family that he worried about?

Back to Daniel. I have to believe that Daniel had some dark times during those three weeks. I wonder if he even felt like he may have been forgotten after fasting and praying for three weeks with no answer from the Lord. I confess, my patience has been short at times, and I have prayed for much shorter durations, and got frustrated and felt like God was silent and not listening to my pleas. I've definitely never fasted for three weeks. But Daniel did, and the whole time the answer to his prayer, the man with the explanation of his confusing vision, was on his way to him. He was fighting to make it to Daniel. Daniel hadn't been forgotten. God was not silent. He had even employed Michael, the archangel, to fight the spiritual battle necessary for Daniel's prayers to be answered.

I've learned things are not always what they seem. I believe I'm naturally more of a pessimistic person, and I tend to go down the worst case scenario spiral in my head, so I'm guilty of saying things to God like, "Where were you on that one?" Or "Don't you even care what is going on here?" But, in the three to four years that I've been keeping a prayer journal, I can go back and see all the things that I've prayed for, and with those 20/20 hindsight glasses trace the moves of God behind the scenes that I could not possibly have understood at the time. In fact, looking back over those journals is sometimes very painful for me because I cringe at my own distrust of the Lord and lack of patience with his plan. I have actually told Travis that all of those notebooks are to be burned when I die. I'm learning to have compassion for the past version of myself because she didn't have the experience that I do now. She didn't know the end of the story. She was in pain, and she was walking in faith the best way she knew how. On this side of that season of suffering, I'm able to say in confidence that God is good, and that even when the circumstances are the darkest and you're drowning in a sea of doubt, things are not what they seem. Romans 8:28 is true and God is working *all things* for the good of those who love him and are called according to his purpose. Who knows, the answer to your prayer may be engaging in some serious spiritual warfare to get to you, just like Daniel's. Keep persevering.

CHAPTER 20

We Are Not Orphans

Within a couple of weeks of Travis' diagnosis something within me began to shift. I began to believe, not just in my head, but also in my heart that God was going to do immeasurable good on behalf of my little family. I had no tangible evidence that anything was going to work out favorably. Travis' treatments were going well, but he was still a long way from being finished; he had several months left to go of daily treatment and a couple more years of oral chemotherapy treatments. There was really no change in circumstance with the children other than DCS was very accommodating to allow our families to stay at our house with the children while Travis was in the hospital. But I felt an unexplainable peace.

I believe it was the "peace that passes understanding" that Paul talks about in Philippians 4. Paul told the Philippians they would experience peace that exceeds anything they could understand when they quit worrying and prayed about everything, telling God what they needed and thanking Him for all He had done. I really had no option other than to quit worrying about the kids because my mind and body couldn't hold the anxiety over both situations. When I refused to let that worry rule my thoughts and my actions and just continued to bring my prayers to God over the situation all the while thanking Him for every blessing I could find, the peace came over me, not all at once, but in slow ripples.

We definitely haven't fought this cancer battle perfectly. We have doubted God's plan. We have seen Him provide, only to doubt that he would come through the next time there was a bump in the road. We've relied on our own strength, rather than turning to God. We have lost sight of blessings and found plenty to complain about.

I've realized I've had many "forgetful Israelite moments" on this cancer journey. I've always been pretty hard on the Israelites in the story of their exodus from Egypt. They saw God work all those miracles that defied scientific odds to rescue them from their 400-year slavery in Egypt only to yell at Moses, saying, "You've brought us out here to die!" when the Egyptians pursued them to the Red Sea. Or when they began complaining about how much better the food in Egypt was right after God miraculously led them across dry ground in the middle of the Red Sea and killed all the Egyptian soldiers who tried to come after them. Until all of this happened, I had a habit of reading those stories and thinking, "Wow, these people are a bunch of forgetful, faithless, ungrateful whiners." Unfortunately, I can put my own spin on each of the stories I just recounted with myself as the forgetful, faithless, ungrateful whiner. It's a good thing God is in the business of progress (sanctification) not perfection. He has been patient, merciful, gracious, and kind to us throughout this journey when we have done nothing to deserve it.

But somehow, just like those Israelites I still manage to fear when life or the Enemy inevitably throws a curveball and messes up my well-laid plans. Those curveballs come in all shapes and sizes. Sometimes they look like health issues, sometimes they look like anxiety over my children's future, sometimes they look like financial difficulty, sometimes they look like the uncertainty that comes along with a world-wide pandemic, and sometimes they look like failure. My friends' curveballs have looked like infertility, miscarriage, divorce, addictions to substances and pornography, and job loss. Life is hard, and the fallen state of this world gives us plenty of opportunity to fear and act like those forgetful Israelites. But have you ever noticed how many times God tells us "Do not fear" through scripture? It is repeated often. I've heard it said many times that it is in the Bible 365 times, enough for every day of the year. So why shouldn't we fear, especially when our circumstances look bleak? Well, God usually follows up the command to not fear with a reminder that He is always with his children.

In Deuteronomy, Moses spends a lot of time giving the Israelites his farewell speech. God has told him he will not be entering the Promised Land with them, and that his time on Earth is almost over. So, with some of the last words he knows that will escape his mouth on this side of eternity he calls Joshua out of the crowd and admonishes him with the words, "Be strong and courageous, for you must go with this people into the land that the Lord swore to their ancestors to give them, and you must divide it among them as their inheritance. The Lord himself goes before you and will be with you; he will never leave you nor forsake you. Do not be afraid; do not be discouraged" (Deuteronomy 31:7-8, NIV).

Just a couple of pages over in my Bible, the Lord himself reminds Joshua of these words three times. In Joshua 1:9 (NIV), God says, "Have I not commanded you? Be strong and courageous. Do not be afraid; do not be discouraged for the Lord your God will be with you wherever you go."

First of all, this is very encouraging to me because the Lord has to use repetition for me to catch on. I notice I get very aggravated when my kids don't catch on to something as quickly as I would like, and I must repeat myself over and over, but I'm humbled when I think about how the Lord usually has to show me a specific scripture in several different ways and in several different places for me to think, "Hmm, maybe I should pay attention to what the Lord is saying here."

Secondly, it's very encouraging to me that Joshua, who had proven to be one of the most faithful of God's people still needed to be reminded not to be afraid or discouraged. Back in the early years of the Israelites' wilderness wanderings, Moses sent 12 spies (one from each tribe) into the Promised Land to scout out the people who lived there, the land, and the cities and fortifications. Out of the 12 spies who went to scout out the land, only two came back with a positive report, Joshua and Caleb. The other 10 spies told the people that the land they scouted would devour its inhabitants and that the people who lived there were giants and the Israelites seemed like grasshoppers compared to them, but Joshua and Caleb declared that the land was an extremely good land, and that the Lord would bring them into it if he was pleased with them.

Joshua and Caleb petitioned the people not to rebel against God and not be afraid of the people of the land because they had God with them. Most of us know the end of the story; the people rebelled anyway and threatened to stone Joshua and Caleb. God declared that none of the Israelites who had seen His miraculous works in the Exodus from Egypt would enter the Promised Land other than Joshua and Caleb. The rest of them would die in the wilderness over the next 40 years for their lack of faith (Numbers 13-14). So, we can see that Joshua's trust and faith in God was strong, but God still felt the need to remind even him to be strong and courageous and not to fear, not once, not twice, but three times.

Joshua went on to demolish the city of Jericho, conquer the Promised Land, and divide the territory up among the tribes just as Moses said he would. He was victorious all around, but it did not mean that the battle didn't come with struggle. God's plan for bringing down Jericho was a strange one to say the least, and Joshua had to take the risk of looking like a fool to the Canaanites and his own people as he led them to march around the city walls every day for a week. But his obedience to God, even when the plan seemed weird, brought about victory. Conquering the Promised Land was also no easy feat. There were many battles to be fought, sin that had to be dealt with, covenants that had to be renewed, literal giants that had to be slayed, and disagreements that had to be worked out, but God was with his people through all of it, just as he had promised he would be, and at the end of Joshua's life his message to the people was, "Now I am about to go the way of all the earth. You know with all your heart and soul that not one of all the good promises the Lord your God gave you has failed. Every promise has been fulfilled; not one has failed" (Joshua 23:14, NIV). Joshua's most pressing concern at the end of his life was that his people remember that their God is with them, that he keeps his word, and that he is trustworthy.

David continues the theme of not being fearful in his "greatest hit" of Psalm 23, "Even though I walk through valley of the shadow of death, I will fear no evil, for you are with me; your rod and your staff, they comfort me. You prepare a table for me in the presence of my enemies. You anoint my head with oil; my cup overflows. Surely goodness and mercy shall follow me all the days of my life, and I shall dwell in the house of the Lord forever" (Psalm 23:4-6, ESV).

Again, David says he is not going to fear evil when he is walking through the darkest valleys of his life because he knows God is with him. He also says that God's "rod and staff" as his shepherd comfort him. Why would these two shepherd's tools be comforting to David? As we know, David himself was a shepherd who took care of his father's sheep. David tells King Saul, "Your servant has been keeping his father's sheep. When a lion or a bear came and carried off a sheep from the flock, I went after it, struck it and rescued the sheep from its mouth. When it turned on me, I seized it by its hair, struck it and killed it" (1 Samuel 17:34-35, NIV). David would have used his rod and staff as the tools to kill the predators and rescue his sheep. So, he has complete faith that God himself will defeat his enemies and rescue him from the dark valley in which he finds himself.

David also says that God prepares a table for him in the presence of his enemies. David's enemy at the time was King Saul. Saul had it out for him. He had tried to kill him twice and he continually pursued him and hunted him down to try to do away with him, but David knew that God would not only rescue him from the dark valley, but that he would also exalt him in the presence of his enemy, the King.

David also says that God anoints his head with oil and his cup overflows. This is a call back to when Samuel anointed David as king, "So Samuel took the horn of oil and anointed him in the presence of his brothers, and from that day on the Spirit of the Lord came powerfully upon David" (1 Samuel 16:13, NIV). I believe David is remembering the day God's Spirit came upon him when he was anointed with oil, and he is comparing himself and the overflow of God's spirit within him to a cup that is overflowing. So, David has realized that as long as he walks with God and is filled with God's presence, he has no need to fear because God will rescue him from the dark valleys, defeat his enemies, and continue to pursue him with goodness and mercy, unlike the spirits of wrath and death that his enemy Saul had pursued him with for years on end.

As with Moses and Joshua, I believe it's important to pay attention to what people choose to say when they know their time is short. People who know their time is short, don't tend to waste their words on fluff. The things they muster the strength to say are the things they want their loved ones to remember. Moses wanted Joshua to know that he needed to be strong and courageous and that he had no reason to fear because God would go with him. Joshua wanted the people to know that their God was a promise keeper, that he was faithful, and that he could be trusted.

John is my favorite gospel. It has been for about five years now. Some of my favorite words in the Bible are in

John's prologue. Don't get me started on the first episode of the second season of the Chosen. Oh my, that whole montage at the end where Jesus is reading from Genesis 1 in the synagogue and John is penning his prologue after the martyr of his brother and the audio goes back and forth between their two voices reading the words of the two books is almost too much for me. I ugly cried my way through it. I can't even type this paragraph without blinking back tears to be able to see the screen. Sorry, rabbit trail, but this sets up my love for John's Gospel. One of the main reasons I love John's Gospel so much is that John gives us five chapters of almost uninterrupted speech from Jesus on the night before his crucifixion. Jesus knew his time was short. Jesus told his betrayer, Judas, "What you're doing, do quickly" (John 13:27, NASB). And Judas leaves the group. When Judas has left, Jesus immediately launches into the words he wants them to remember. In John 16:33, Jesus basically says to his disciples, "I have told you these things so that you may have peace. You will have suffering in this world. Be courageous! I have conquered the world." So, what are the things Jesus told them that would give them peace and allow them to live courageously through suffering? He had repeatedly told them throughout John chapters 14-16 that he would be with them. How would Jesus be with them if he knew he was walking toward the cross to die and then would be ascending back to the father? (John 14:1-4). The answer is the Holy Spirit.

- In John 14:15-26, Jesus promised that God would give them another counselor who is the Spirit of Truth. He promised that he would not leave them as orphans and that the Holy Spirit would teach them all things and remind them of everything he had told them.

- In John 15:26, Jesus promised that the Counselor, the Spirit of Truth, would testify about him.
- In John 16:7-15, Jesus gives them a real mind-bender and says that it is better for him to go away because if he doesn't go the Counselor would not come. He also says that the Counselor will convict the world about sin, righteousness, and judgment. He says again that the Spirit of Truth would guide them into all truth.

And just as Joshua wanted the Israelites to know that God had kept all his good promises, and not one of them had failed, Jesus wants us to know that he can be trusted to keep his promises as well. In John 14:1-3 (ESV) Jesus says, "Let not your heart be troubled. Believe in God; believe also in me. In my Father's house are many rooms. If it were not so, would I have told you that I am going to prepare a place for you? And if I go and prepare a place for you, I will come again and take you to myself, so that where I am you may be also." In this passage, Jesus is telling his disciples that they don't have to fear because he will keep his promise to return for them.

I must believe that the Holy Spirit's power and presence in our lives is more significant than I have given him credit for throughout my life. The older I get, the more suffering I see, and the darker the world becomes, the more I believe that we can't do this Christian life in our own strength, understanding, power, and righteousness. I more and more believe that Jesus's last words to his disciples in John 14-16 carry heavier weight than I have assigned them, especially since Jesus told his boys that it is better for him to go, so that the Counselor could come. This gift of God's presence dwelling in believers is significant in many ways.

Just as Moses wanted Joshua to know that he needed to be strong and courageous and to not fear because God was with him, Jesus wants us to know the same thing. We can be strong and courageous because the Holy Spirit is with us and in us. We are not orphans. We are dearly loved children of God who have all the tools we need to live lives of godliness through our salvation which was purchased by Jesus on the cross (John 14:6), the power of the Holy Spirit (John 16:7-15), the truth of Scripture (John 14:15-26), and the love of our community of believers (John 15:9-17).

CHAPTER 21

Joyful in Hope &
Patient in Tribulation

One of my greatest shortcomings in my Christian walk is setting aside a specific time just to pray. I do believe I chat with God throughout my day. Most of the time when I'm totally messing something up or just need more patience. I do teach teenagers and have two young children so you can imagine how much patience I need. I blame some of it on my attention issues but it's just filling my schedule up that I go from sunup to sundown scheming to have as much fun as possible. That all changes when you are locked up in a hospital for over a month with your life on the line. Suddenly you have a great amount of time on your hands. I was so blessed with visitors, most of which wanted to pray with me. As one would imagine, I've never prayed so much in my life. As life has returned to some sense of normalcy, I've fallen back into my old habits. I still pray throughout the day, but I don't stop often enough and give my full attention to the LORD. I've found that if I have a physical and/or visual reminder, I am more likely to remember to take that vital moment and converse with the Almighty.

I changed my lock screen and background photo to a picture of Whitney (lock screen) and my kids (background). I purchased a cross necklace as a reminder. Recently Whitney gave me a list of items she wants me to pray for and I keep that list in my pocket. Whitney trusts me to pray for her. She trusts my communication with our Father. That is a huge responsibility and blessing. God wants our trust. He made himself vulnerable in the form of his Son and died an excruciating, embarrassing death to give us the ability to communicate with him.

***

God typically speaks to me through repetition of His word. I will see or hear the same scripture in different unrelated places. In August of 2018, the scripture repeated everywhere I turned was Romans 12:12 (ESV), "Be joyful in hope, patient in tribulation, and constant in prayer."

I got a new prayer notebook that month to start a new school year, and hopefully keep my journaling habit on track with the busyness of the school year, football season, and raising two toddlers looming overhead. The notebook was a 7 by 10 inch spiral bound notebook with simple college-ruled white paper inside. I liked it because it had a folder pocket in the middle of the notebook. In the folder pocket, I kept my church prayer list, a prayer calendar for Travis, a prayer calendar for the kids, and a stack of notecards that had prayers written on them that I offered up to the Lord over and over. The front of the notebook was pale pink, like a baby's girl's blanket. I knew I wanted a theme verse for that season to write on the cover of the new notebook, so I prayed as I began looking for the perfect one. Romans 12 felt like the right spot to look. As I skimmed Paul's familiar words about the marks of a Christian, verse 12 jumped off the page, "Be joyful in hope, patient in tribulation, and constant in prayer." I knew that word was for me, and that I needed it for the weeks and months to come.

I had no idea that the road I was journeying down was about to get even rockier than it already was. All I knew was that I was really spiraling downward into a pit of depression and anxiety over our kids' future. Just a few weeks prior to buying my new journal, I sent an email to my coworkers asking them to pray that we would believe God's plans for the kids were good, that we would trust in His goodness to our very core, that we would continually have passion for the assignment to care for Hailee and Daniel and to see the fruit in it, that we would run the race with endurance because we had never felt so spiritually, emotionally, or physically drained in all our lives.

In the weeks and months to come, I would see how perfect Romans 12:12 was for the season of life. I would need to find my joy in the hope that only Jesus provides, and stand my ground there, where the hope could be found because as badly as I wanted a breakthrough right then on my timing and in accordance with my plans, the break- through didn't come like I wanted it to. In fact, the world only got darker. I had to continually re-gospel myself during those fall days, telling myself that even if everything collapsed around me, the battle had already been won on the cross.

I assumed the patience I required was for the tribulation of enduring the uncertainty of my kids' future. I didn't realize another major tribulation lay in wait for my little family just a few weeks down the road. My journals are full of impatient pleas for God to work miracles for the kids' unimaginable good *right now*. My timeline didn't line up exactly with God's. "I wanted what I wanted like six months ago, please God."

Constant in prayer. That is so much easier when your life is in the balance. You're so very aware of your lack of control and smallness. Constant in prayer was Paul's one bullet point that seemed a little more natural in this season of life for me.

- I used a black Sharpie marker to write the scripture on the pale pink cover of my notebook, and then I wrote my name in a pale pink marker on the first page of the notebook along with a few more verses about God's faithfulness to answer prayer in hopes that these words would keep me constant in prayer when I didn't see the mountains being thrown into the sea.
- The very next day my boss sent his daily email to the faculty and staff and the subject line said, "constant in prayer." The message was all about Romans 12:12. I continued seeing and hearing messages from scripture about persistence in prayer. Each time I would write it down as a reminder of what God was telling me.
- One of our alumni spoke to a group of students about a summer mission trip to Africa, and she told the parable of the persistent widow and her continual pleading for justice.
- My middle school Bible class was learning about

the book of Acts. We read about how the
Christians devoted themselves daily to prayer.

- My friend Britney posted a verse from the
  Psalms on her Instagram account that jumped
  out at me, "Every morning I will explain my
  need to him. Every evening I will move my soul
  toward him. Every waking hour I will worship
  only him" (Psalm 55:17, TPT).

That couldn't have explained "constant prayer" any
more thoroughly. The next day, I opened my Jesus Calling
devotional to find the same verse on the day's reading.
Repeatedly, God was reminding me to stay close to him, to
talk to him, to be with him. He knew the battle we would be
facing. He knows my tendency to fret, worry, and expect the
worst. He knew I would need to have the mind of Christ for
the coming days, weeks, and months.

I have found C.S. Lewis' quote about prayer to be true,
"I pray because I can't help myself. I pray because I'm helpless. I pray because the need flows out of me all the time,
waking and sleeping. It doesn't change God. It changes
me."[1] Especially the part about prayer changing the person,
not God. The seasons in my life that have been marked by a
consistent prayer life have been the seasons when I was the
most gracious, compassionate, loving, and slow to anger. In
short, prayer helps conform me to the character of God.
Prayer also helps me trust God more, act in greater obedience, and walk in hopeful anticipation of seeing God's
power.

I used to pride myself on being able to persevere, to
endure. I was a swimmer when I was a kid. I loved the

summers I spent under the sun in the Albertville rec center pool. The smell of a freshly chlorinated pool still smells like home to me. When I was a swimmer, I most excelled in the "tough events," the ones no one else seemed to like to swim; butterfly, individual medleys, and long freestyle races. I wore my excellence in these categories like a badge of honor. I was tough, I was strong, and I could persevere through the hard stuff. As an adult I coached cross-country for 7 years. The hot August days and hilly terrain in Southern Middle Tennessee give plenty of opportunity for a cross-country coach to preach endurance to young runners who are ready to give up. We also wore our grit as a badge of honor; heck, we even put it on a tee shirt, "our sport is your sport's punishment." How's that for being tough, strong, persevering? It's October of 2021, and I'm wondering if I should throw away my cross-country tees and swimming medals and remove my "badge of honor."

I'm tired, I'm weak, and I'm feeling like I'm at the end of my rope. I feel like all the perseverance has been drained out of me over the last four-and-a-half years.

- It started with a long season of being new parents to not just one kid, but two under the age of two. That is tough enough but add on top of the neglect our babies had endured and the trauma they experienced in being uprooted from all they had known and being plopped down in the home of two strangers.
- Once we were all settled as a little family unit and life seemed to be moving along at a more comfortable pace, we experienced the emotional

whiplash of the threat of our children being removed from our home and placed back with their biological parents.

- When all the hope looked lost for our little family unit staying together, Travis' diagnosis knocked us down like a linebacker that evaded the coverage of the offensive linemen and hit us right in the blindside.

- Before Travis could even get out of treatment, our beloved RCA hit a low that had never happened in the ministry before. The Board of Directors began to be worried that our school would not even survive.

- God worked miracles, and when I say miracles, I mean big ones! Travis was declared cancer-free in March of 2019, and the kids were adopted in July of 2019! RCA's Board of Directors made many strategic shifts that have put the ministry in a safer financial position than it has ever been before. Everything was resolved. All that I had prayed for, that I had poured my tears out for was accomplished. God had made it all happen in his kindness. Whew, I could check my "big test of faith" off the list. I had endured my season of suffering and had a testimony for the glorification of God and the upbuilding of his Kingdom. Now, I could rest from my trials for a minute, then I would help Travis write this book and tell people all about the good things God did, and how He is trustworthy even in the darkest of times because He is working even when we don't see it.

- Then September 19, 2019, happened. I woke up and couldn't move. I was in so much pain from the top of my neck to my lower back. The pain made it hard to raise my voice, go to the bathroom, and even to swallow. After a month or so, I was diagnosed with degenerative disc disease. The pain continued at intense levels for 11 months, moving around in my body and causing different sensations like numbness, tingling, burning skin, and more.

- The COVID-19 pandemic hit March of 2020, and Travis still had several months of oral chemotherapy medications to go. The stress of the pandemic, schooling virtually, and anxiety over Travis' health was suffocating at times.

- Meanwhile my pain never subsided. There were days that were better than others, but overall, I was in pain every minute of every day. Fast forward to July/August of 2021, my pain reached new levels and then I was hit out of the blue with dizziness that has not subsided in 10 weeks at this point. In the last few weeks, I have lost some of my gross motor function, ability to balance, and walk long distances without stabilization. I have been to at least six doctors, made a trip to the ER, had a CT scan of my brain, four MRIs, and vials upon vials of blood work done with still no answers for my condition.

And God keeps talking to me about endurance. He did it again today. I felt the urge to open my Bible app this afternoon. I just had this feeling from the Holy Spirit that there was something waiting for me there. And there was. The same thing I have been hearing from the Lord for the last two months: endure. The verse of the day read: "For everything that was written in the past was written to teach us, so that through the endurance taught in the Scriptures and the encouragement they provide we might have hope" (Romans 15:4, NIV).

Those are Paul's words to the Romans, near the end of his letter. He is encouraging the readers of the letter to stay in the scriptures (the only ones they've had at the time were the Old Testament because the New Testament was being written as they lived) because they give hope through the endurance taught in them and the encouragement they provide.

Paul knew their lives would be hard. He knew they would endure suffering. He knew life would not just be one major crisis or test of faith and done, but a series of crises, seasons of suffering, and seasons of rejoicing, a life-long journey toward sanctification that would require constant refreshing from the Living Word.

When I read today's verse of the day, I smirked a little to myself and told the Lord that I heard him. Just like I've heard him repeatedly in the last few weeks when He put 2 Thessalonians 3:5 (NIV) in front of my face, "May the Lord direct your hearts to God's love and Christ's endurance." And then again, a few days later when Hebrews 12:1 was the theme verse for my daily Bible study, "Therefore, since we are surrounded by so great a cloud of witnesses, let us also lay aside every weight, and the sin which clings so closely, and let us run with endurance the race that is set before for us." And the day after that, again the theme verse of my Bible study was endurance in James 1:3 (NIV), "because you know that the testing of your faith produces endurance."

The picture I keep getting is one of my faith muscles being pushed beyond what I believed was possible. I have had moments as an athlete when my body responded in competition in ways that were beyond what I thought was possible due to the endurance I had gained from practice. Hebrews 11:1 defines faith as the confidence in what we hope for and assurance about what we do not see. Faith doesn't come naturally to us in the 21st century. We can get evidence for anything we want with the swipe of a finger across the device that lives in our pockets, heck we don't even have to swipe; we can just ask Siri. No, faith must be practiced. It must be stretched. It must be pushed in order to grow, and it is important to grow in faith because as the Hebrew writer continues, "without faith it is impossible to please God, because anyone who comes to him must believe that he exists and that he rewards those who earnestly seek him" (Hebrews 11:16, NIV).

I realize now that what I thought was endurance and perseverance really wasn't, because endurance and perseverance don't come when you're doing the things you excel at in your own strength or even when you're doing the things you enjoy. Endurance and perseverance grow in the fire of trials and suffering. Going back to James, in context, he writes the following about suffering, trials, endurance, and maturity in the faith:

Consider it pure joy, my brothers and sisters, whenever you encounter various trials, knowing that the testing of your faith produces endurance. And let endurance have its perfect result, so that you may be mature and complete, lacking in nothing (James 1:2-4, NASB).

So basically, not getting what we want, when we want it builds endurance and perseverance, and the finished work of endurance is maturity in our faith or a growth of trust in God, his goodness, and his power, presence, and plan for us.

Paul says a very similar statement about endurance, suffering, and hope in Romans 5:3-4 (ESV):

Not only that, but we rejoice in our sufferings, knowing that suffering produces endurance, and endurance produces character, and character produces hope, and hope does not put us to shame, because God's love has been poured into our hearts through the Holy Spirit who has been given to us.

Both statements remind me of a song by Hillsong United. The song is called "Another in the Fire." It is in reference to the fourth man in the fire with Shadrach, Meshach and Abednego in the book of Daniel. These three young men were not saved from the suffering of the difficult decision to follow God amid persecution. They made the decision not to bow to the "things of this world" even though they knew the consequence would be that they would be thrown into the furnace. But God was with them in the furnace. He saved them from death and brought glory to His name in the process. The part of the song that makes my eyes well up with tears every time is, "And should I ever need reminding [of] how good you've been to me, I'll count the joy come every battle 'cause I know that's where you'll be."[2]

Those words make me cry because I've found them to be true, and oh how I wish they were not. The times in my life when I've felt God's presence the most were in the seasons of suffering. C.S. Lewis said it too in his book *The Problem of Pain:* "God whispers to us in our pleasures, speaks to us in our conscience, but shouts in our pains; it is his megaphone to rouse a deaf world."[3] Lewis is absolutely correct. The times in my life when I've heard God's messages most clearly were in the trials when I was the weakest and I had to rely on His strength. Paul writes to the Corinthians about this in his second letter. He states, "Three times I pleaded with the Lord about this, that it should leave me (a thorn in the flesh). But he said to me, 'My grace is sufficient for you, for my power is made perfect in weakness.' Therefore, I will boast all the more gladly of my weaknesses, so that the power of Christ may rest upon me. For the sake of Christ, then, I am content with weaknesses, insults, hardships, persecutions, and calamities. For when I am weak, then I am strong'" (2 Corinthians 12:8-10). Paul is counting the joy in his battle against that thorn in his flesh, whatever it was, because he knew that in his endurance, trust, and obedience through the strength of the Holy Spirit and not his own, God would be glorified.

The older I get, and the more of these seasons I endure through the strength of the Holy Spirit, the easier it is to hope, to expectantly await a move of the Lord and the easier it is to trust that God is good and that He is for me. It's that faith muscle. It has memory, just like your body's muscles have memory. Your body's muscles hold memories of the ways they have been trained to act and react in physical situations like sports practices until what was once difficult and had to be practiced continually became routine. Your body becomes mature in that movement. This is the same thing Paul tells us about faith. It isn't easy. In fact, growing in faith and trust in the Lord and letting go of my comfort and control is the toughest thing I have ever experienced.

ENDNOTES

[1] C.S. Lewis. AZQuotes.com, Wind and Fly LTD, 2022. https://www.azquotes.com/quote/877336, accessed March 16, 2022.

[2] Lyrics.com, STANDS4 LLC, 2022. "Another in the Fire Lyrics." Accessed March 16, 2022. https://www.lyrics.com/lyric/36277432/Hillsong+United.

[3] C.S. Lewis, "The Problem of Pain," *The C.S. Lewis Signature Classics*. (New York: Harper Collins, 2017), 604.

CHAPTER 22

His Faithful Love Endures Forever

It is January 1, 2020 and I'm getting ready to watch a day of football. My kids are "picking up" their toys that they've scattered all over the house. Home Alone 2 is on as I await kickoff for my beloved Crimson Tide. The last year or so dating back to October 2018 has been a wild ride. I was told that I was in remission last March. I find myself thinking about that moment a lot which immediately takes me back to sitting in the infusion room with others suffering from the dreaded "C" word. I would say that nurses are some of the most underappreciated people on the planet. Even now I could call a hotline number in case of an emergency and get personal care. I've begun my fourth cycle of eight in the maintenance phase of my chemotherapy. For the first 15 days I take ATRA twice a day and then the remaining 75 days I do a daily and weekly dose of two different oral chemo meds. There is hope that I might come off all meds in March as the current chemo does a number on my liver enzymes driving them higher than they need to be. I haven't had unbearable, noticeable side effects so I've been blessed. That doesn't mean that fear doesn't *creep in every so often. When I have nightmares that aren't even associated with cancer, I awake covered in sweat with chemotherapy bone pain throughout my body. I have to mentally, along with breathing techniques, walk through the steps of reality through the 3-2-1 mindfulness technique to bring me back to an awareness through the senses of my actual situation. First, I start off by listing 3 things I can see, then 3 things I can hear, and then 3 things I can touch. I repeat these steps with two new things of each and finally finish with one new thing I randomly notice. I do not want to live in fear but there are certain triggers that open the floodgates of emotions. Whether it is a smell, location, or a taste it can be overwhelming. I've learned to share with someone when I feel this way. That practice has not come easy as I don't like the whiff of negativity, but it is necessary to not be crushed. Along with breathing techniques I also try to be in the moment. Let those emotions come but don't let them isolate you from what is actually happening. I also use the counting method that goes like this: 3. What is something I can see? 2. What is something I can smell? 1. What is something I can touch? This has been very beneficial and grounding.*

As we have seen throughout history and especially in the last few years, fear can be toxic, and it can cripple us. There are ideals in any given situation, and our personal continuum between ideal and unacceptable has a huge impact on how we see life. Unhealthy ideals can be described as "all or nothing," "black or white," and "perfect or failure." Either it's the greatest day ever because everything is going the way I want or it's the worst day because everything is not going the way I want. There should be levels and most days should be in the middle between the extremes.

Warrior poet, brother in Christ and friend, Lonnie Jones illustrates this idea with the thinness of a piece of paper. For some people, the difference between terrible and great is super thin and that is unhealthy. When the difference between the two should be like walls on either side of a room with varying degrees between ideal and unacceptable. Lonnie also uses the "favorite food" illustration by asking the questions, "What is your favorite food?" followed by, "What is the worst possible thing you can eat?" Let's say the first answer is ice cream and the second is broccoli. So, in the perfectionist view everything that isn't ice cream is broccoli. Is spaghetti closer to ice cream or broccoli? There are lots of choices between ideal and unacceptable.

It is terrifying to hear you have cancer or any health issue that could result in death. I don't wish it on anyone, but you do have choices to make pertaining to your attitude. I wish I would've taken a little more time to process it in that moment. If I had to do it over again, I might mourn a little longer. I believe because of my relationship with God and the wonderful community of believers who surrounded me I was able to combat fear of the unknown. God tells us in the Bible 365 times, "Do not fear." As Whitney mentioned earlier, God's repetition equates importance. Trusting God is a simple thought but difficult in practice especially when it seems all the signs point in the opposite direction. We as believers must be signposts pointing the way to the one true God and his consistent nature.

***

God spent the last six months of 2020 reminding me

repeatedly about what his character is like. It started in the summer. I was reading a children's devotional book with the kids one morning at breakfast, and the words gracious, compassionate, slow to anger, and abounding in faithful love jumped off the page at me. I put it on the letter board that sits by our kitchen table, and we talked about those characteristics of God every day. The Bible Project then released a video series last fall on the character of God as He describes himself to Moses in Exodus 34:6-7. I get an email in my inbox every time they release a new video, so for six weeks, God reminded me through my email inbox about what his character is truly like: gracious, compassionate, slow to anger, and abounding in faithful love. This was important because I was beginning to be bitter toward Him in this season of suffering. There have been many times I've reminded myself of who God really is and how He has been gracious, compassionate, slow to anger, and abounding in faithful love toward me in the past when everything looked dark, and there seemed to be no way forward. *Ugh*, I give the Israelites in the wilderness such a hard time because of all the miracles they witnessed, but they still managed to question God's goodness and his plan for their lives, but I find myself doing the same thing all the time.

I've not written anything in this book for a long time. Mostly, because I want to be able to wrap things up with a nice bow for you. I wanted to say look at what God has done! He answered our prayers, removed all our suffering, did all the miracles, but I felt like I wouldn't be telling you the whole truth if I left it at that. The truth is I am still in a season of suffering and weakness. I think the motive behind that is I want to "protect" God's character.

I remember when Travis was in the hospital, I had a hard time posting an update on his health if it didn't end on a high note. There were many highs and lows during the months of his treatment, and many people wanted to stay informed about his condition and how they could pray. I took on the role of Public Relations Manager. I managed the Facebook updates and messages and felt responsible for helping everyone feel like their "prayers were working." On days that we got news that wasn't good like: you have a brain bleed, or you need to skip a treatment because this is too hard on your body, or we're not sure if you'll get to go home for Thanksgiving because your blood counts are too low; I would just wait to post any updates until the doctor had better news. I see now that was out of my desire to protect everyone's attitude toward God and his character in Travis' season of suffering. I wasn't just serving as Travis' main communicator with the outside world; I was trying to be God's PR manager too.

I'm beginning to understand that God doesn't need my PR skills to protect His name and his character. He is fully capable of doing that Himself. I am totally unqualified for that position even though I do have a degree in PR. Ha! But I can tell you this, even in this season of suffering, God has been good. He has been with me. I pray for my healing every day. I don't just sit back in victimized silence accepting this unnamed condition as my lot in life. I am asking every day just like the persistent widow that Jesus talks about in the gospel of Luke. But I also say every day, even if this is my thorn, there is nowhere else to go because He has the words of life, and I'm going to stand my ground where hope can be found (John 6:68).

I urge you in your seasons of trial and suffering to dig in. Satan hates it when we do that. Even in your pain, turn on the worship music and sing it loud even if it is through tears. I daily hang on to this idea from Matt Chandler, the pastor of The Village Church in Texas. He often says in his sermons that when Satan squeezes and worship comes out, rather than his desired outcome of our rejection of God and his goodness, the dark forces of this world get a gut punch.

It's ok to not be ok, don't lie to yourself about how you feel. You don't have to put on a strong face for others to be God's PR manager. You for sure don't have to put on a strong face for God. He knows how you feel. Read the Psalms; David has some words with the Lord over his circumstances. My favorite prophet Jeremiah even tells God at one point that God has tricked him! (Jeremiah 20:7). Tell God how you feel and what you desire; this builds a relationship with Him. He may give you your desire, and he may not, or he may say not yet; you need to build some endurance and strengthen that faith muscle. A lack of truthfulness about what is going on in your head will give Satan a foothold in the spiritual battle for your mind and heart.

Stay in scripture. You must be in the Word to recognize lies when they make their way into your thoughts. Take your thoughts captive as Paul says. Just stop and recognize the things that go through your mind. Are they mean? Are they negative? Are they accusatory against yourself or God? Are they fearful? None of this is from the Lord. Write those thoughts down and battle them with truth from scripture. The Bible is God's Word, as the Hebrew writer says, "it is living and active" and it provides hope for when there is no reason to hope in the darkness of this world (Hebrews 4:12).

Finally, when you're trapped in a thought cycle in your mind, tell someone else who loves the Lord and is grounded in scripture what is going through your head. Sometimes, you just need someone else's input to stop the cycle. I'm holding on to the hope for miracles again. I've seen the Lord do it before, but even if He doesn't, He is still good.

CHAPTER 23

Get Busy Living

Every event has a filter now. I don't believe I'd call it the Cancer filter but it's something that every event, if pondered long enough, filters through. It can happen when a huge, cold rain drop finds its way down the back of my raincoat on a football field on a Friday night, or when I feel the cool breeze on the sandy seashore. I've had the thought while being engulfed by the humidity of Summer camp and playing in the snow on the hilltop. The reminder that this battle isn't over. There is a tremendous comfort that I find in Jesus that the war has already been won. Even in the face of that, I find a fleeting dread though it never stays very long, thankfully. It's a reminder physically that Cancer can always come back. Sometimes it's a Facebook post like the one today about a guy who was younger than me who passed from lung cancer. I try to avoid clicking the link that leads to his profile, but I do. There he is with his three young children. His posts from just a few days prior had such a positive attitude. The weight of "why" comes scratching and clawing back to sit squarely on my shoulders. Not the weight of "why did this *happen to me?" but rather, "why do I get to live?" To that last question, I don't know the concrete answer to it. My response is to live life to the fullest. To squeeze every ounce of goodness from it like a rung-out rag.*

The movie "Shawshank Redemption" is a movie classic. A movie classic that I've never watched from start to finish. Please don't put this book down as I don't mean any disrespect. I've probably seen the entire movie, just in bits and pieces, jumbled up in between flipping through the channels. For some reason it just never seems to be at the beginning. There is a quote that I'm reminded of when I think about the fact that I'm still here on this earth. "Get busy living or get busy dying."[1]

The main character gets emotional talking about what he was going to do when he got out of prison. It involves the ocean, a hotel, and the beach. There were times I didn't know if I'd leave Huntsville Hospital with air in my lungs, but honestly none of us know what tomorrow holds. Sure, when I was "stuck" up there I did think about getting to go back to Maywood Christian Camp or Challenge Youth Conference, but where I wanted to be was in my own bed as close to my wife as possible. I wanted to adopt my kids, I wanted to go to the football playoffs and win another championship as head coach of the Knights. I wanted to taste good food and Dr. Pepper again, in moderation. I wanted to ride around with the windows down and show off my drum solo skills on the steering wheel like Ben Hayes' older brother Dale when he rocked the mullet and drove the firebird. I wanted to play in a golf scramble after not playing golf for two decades and not come in last. I wanted to write a book, make stupid videos, and try really hard at podcasting. Those last few things I didn't even know I wanted to do but I did them because during those times I looked for reasons to quit, God replied with "get busy living."

I took my own advice to get busy living. On September 26, 2021, I returned to my first live college football game since the weekend prior to my diagnosis. I got a lift from Coach Whitworth and his son/former RCA football player Marcus down to Tuscaloosa for the Tide's game hosting Southern Mississippi. It was reminiscent of the trip that Coach Whitworth encouraged me to become a foster parent. It was a beautiful September day. Just warm enough to work up a sweat but not miserable.

On one side of my poster boards, I wrote the familiar gag of "Let This Be a Sign" that I had recreated several times over the years for different events I had attended. On the other side I wrote in poorly drawn black marker "80 + Leukemia Treatments to be here." That number always shocks me and I have to remind myself that it actually happened. I also could not pass up the opportunity to write BenandTravis.com in red marker. Upon seeing the signage, my kids were not going to be happy until they too had left their mark. Hailee wrote "Roll" on the bottom right corner and Daniel wrote "Tide" up the right side of the poster board. I blamed the entire poor writing on my kids when I was asked what the sign read upon arriving in Tuscaloosa. To Coach and Marcus' credit, they were more than happy to let me walk the Crimson clad streets and around the stadium with my sign. As usual I got my fair share of odd stares and questions. I even got asked to pose for a picture. Everyone was in such good spirits for gameday. Thanks to my awesome buddy Will Myhan, I had a great seat in the endzone. It was hard to believe I was really there. I had worn my custom crimson jersey. Number 83 and my last name in white. I had added a "2021 Rose Bowl" patch to the jersey. I completed the ensemble with my player issued, white crown, black bill, Rose Bowl cap from Alabama's playoff victory over Notre Dame from the previous January. I was a kid again even though I was the oldest of our trio with Will and one of his youth group members who is actually a Vanderbilt fan. Vanderbilt as you may remember is where we were the Saturday before my diagnosis. The sun was going down just as the opening kickoff was kicked and Alabama's Jameson Williams returned it for a touchdown. As he broke tackles and spun his way to the end zone there was an older lady behind me who was using her two hands on my shoulders to show her excitement. I'm sure glad it didn't take Williams long to return it because I might not have survived. It was a great way to start because it seemed like we were all there to party anyway. She must have seen the Leukemia side of my sign because she began to ask questions about my journey and ceased to beat on me, thankfully. At some point during the game my "Let This Be A Sign" poster flashed across the television screen because Ben Hayes sent me a screen shot. It was a great evening with awesome people. I'm truly blessed.

At some point, I had to return to the stadium, and I had to return to the men's restroom at a stadium full of people. After a great ride home with great company, I had to calm down to try and go to sleep. I didn't go to sleep until 3 AM that night partly because it is a long ride back from Tuscaloosa. The other reason it was hard to doze off was I knew what awaited. I was right. I had a nightmare of walking into the restroom at Bryant-Denny stadium and my Cancer scare beginning all over again. I awoke from that nightmare with the reassurance that it was over, and I don't have to live in that state of fear of never coming home. I have that reassurance because of Jesus.

We all have an expiration date. Whether you believe in a life after this one or not. Your day is coming. My day is coming. Your pet's day is coming. As a person who has grieved incredibly, gut wrenchingly, surprisingly hard over the loss of a dog, I know that is a low blow. The point is the day is coming when you will leave the cares of this life behind you. All that will matter is did you care for the right things. Cancer is tough, being a foster parent is more difficult in my opinion, but with it, as every circumstance in life comes perspective. I don't believe God gave me Cancer, but He did give me perspective. I've been changed forever. I continue to change. I'm not a pillar of faith and I bounce between extremes, but my hope is the pendulum swings a little less extreme these days. The things that keep me awake at night are different. Yes, the dread of Cancer comes and goes like a wave. More importantly, if I never wake to see another sunrise did the people around me see a little of the Almighty in this earthen vessel? When death rears its ugly face may I be found with a smile, a wink, and zero contempt in my heart. Amen.

ENDNOTES

[1] Darabont, Frank. 1994. The Shawshank Redemption. United States: Columbia Pictures.

Credits

Scripture quotations marked (KJV) are from the King James Version of the Bible.

Scripture quotations marked (ESV) are taken from ESV® Bible (The Holy Bible, English Standard Version®). ESV® Text Edition: 2016. Copyright © 2001 by Crossway

Scripture quotations marked with (NASB) are taken from the New American Standard Bible®, Copyright © 1960, 1971, 1977, 1995 by The Lockman Foundation. All rights reserved.

Scripture quotations marked (NIV) are taken from THE HOLY BIBLE, NEW INTERNATIONAL VERSION®, NIV® Copyright © 1973, 1978, 1984, 2011 by Biblica, Inc.® Used by permission. All rights reserved worldwide.

Scripture quotations marked (NKJV) are from the New